Beekeeping for beekeepers: a practical guide

Don Brown

ISBN 9798878896863

DEDICATION

To my father, the ultimate beekeeper.

CONTENTS

Part 1

Knowing Bees and the Hive

INTRO

Congratulations on embarking on this incredible journey into the fascinating world of beekeeping! This book is your key to unlocking the secrets of these remarkable creatures and becoming a successful, responsible apiarist.

Within these pages, you'll embark on a buzzing adventure, discovering the rich history of beekeeping, the intricate social structures of the hive, and the vital role bees play in our ecosystem. You'll learn the language of the bees, decipher their dances, and become adept at reading the signs of a healthy, thriving colony.

But this journey isn't just about acquiring knowledge; it's about becoming a guardian, a provider, and a steward of nature's wonders. By choosing beekeeping, you've chosen a sustainable and incredibly rewarding activity. You'll witness firsthand the delicate balance of nature, the power of community, and the pure joy of witnessing new life blossom.

Part 1 lays the foundation, introducing you to the marvelous honeybee, their anatomy, social systems, and the essential equipment you'll need to start your apiary. You'll learn to assemble your hive, source healthy bees, and ensure their safety and well-being.

Part 2 takes you through the seasons of the beekeeper, guiding you through spring inspections, managing summer honey production, and preparing your hives for winter's rest. You'll learn to spot potential problems, prevent disease, and ensure your bees thrive throughout the year.

Ready to expand your horizons? Part 3 delves into advanced beekeeping practices. You'll discover how to create new colonies, explore the exciting world of niche bee products, and tackle challenges with confidence. We'll equip you with resources and support networks to ensure your apiary flourishes year after year.

This book is your companion, your guide, and your cheerleader. With each page, you'll gain the knowledge and confidence to navigate the world of beekeeping, contributing to a sustainable future and witnessing the magic of these tiny yet essential creatures.

So, don your bee suit, open your mind, and prepare to be amazed! Your beekeeping journey begins now.

CHAPTER 1

THE MARVELOUS HONEYBEE

Prepare to embark on a buzzing journey into the world of the honeybee! In this opening chapter, we'll peel back the layers of these fascinating creatures, uncovering their rich history, vital role in the ecosystem, and the intricate workings within their tiny bodies and bustling colonies.

Join us as we travel through time, exploring the remarkable history of beekeeping, a practice dating back millennia. We'll delve into the fascinating relationship between humans and bees, showcasing how beekeeping has evolved and the cultural significance these incredible creatures hold around the world.

But understanding their historical connection isn't enough. We'll dive deeper, exploring why bees are truly crucial for the health of our planet. As the primary pollinators, they play an irreplaceable role in maintaining biodiversity and ensuring food security. Their impact goes far beyond honey production, and understanding their importance motivates us to become responsible stewards of their well-being.

Next, we'll shrink down to the size of a bee and explore their amazing anatomy and physiology. Discover the secrets hiding beneath their exoskeletons, from the powerhouses that fuel their flight to the specialized tools they use for collecting nectar and defending their hive. By understanding their body's marvels, we can better appreciate their resilience and adaptations.

But a single bee is just one piece of the puzzle. In the final section, we'll unravel the mysteries of colony structure and social behavior. Witness the complex hierarchy, the remarkable communication systems, and the fascinating division of labor within the hive. These social marvels paint a stunning picture of cooperation and collective intelligence, inspiring us to respect and understand the natural order of the bee world.

A buzzing journey through time: the history of beekeeping

Before we delve into the intricate world of beekeeping, a moment to consider their long and winding history alongside humanity is valuable. This history stretches back millennia, weaving a rich tapestry of ancient traditions, groundbreaking discoveries, and ultimately, the profound significance of these seemingly tiny creatures for our planet. While excitement abounds when exploring the world of bees, understanding their historical journey lays the foundation for appreciating their intricate lives and our role in ensuring their continued well-being.

Our bond with bees stretches back further than recorded history, whispering in the leaves and buzzing in the pollen-laden air. Imagine our prehistoric ancestors, their lives guided by intuition and the hunt for sustenance, stumbling upon a hidden treasure unlike any other. Nestled within a weathered tree hollow or hidden amongst sun-drenched rocks, they would have encountered a marvel - a honeycomb, overflowing with golden, gooey sweetness. This primal encounter, estimated to have occurred over 8,000 years ago, marked the beginning of a remarkable shared story, one that transcended mere resource acquisition and blossomed into a deep-rooted relationship with these fascinating creatures.

The initial surprise at discovering this natural bounty likely transformed into awe as our ancestors witnessed the bees themselves – tiny bundles of energy flitting between delicate blossoms and the honeycomb's intricate waxen chambers. Curiosity morphed into cautious observation, eventually leading to understanding and a rudimentary form of honey collecting. The sweetness extracted from these hives wasn't just a delicious treat; it provided valuable energy, especially during harsh winters or lean seasons.

However, over time, this interaction evolved beyond mere collection. Evidence of this deepening bond can be found in ancient cave paintings across continents, depicting individuals scaling cliffs and braving dangers in

3

pursuit of this natural treasure. These early beekeepers weren't just driven by the sweetness; they recognized the vital role bees played in their survival. The delicate dance of pollination, ensuring the flourishing of plants and crops, became increasingly evident. This realization fostered a shift from simply collecting honey to actively protecting and nurturing beehives. The bond deepened, fueled not just by sustenance but also by a growing understanding and appreciation for the complex social structures and remarkable behaviors of these tiny marvels.

Fast forward through the bustling corridors of time, and we find beekeeping woven into the fabric of ancient civilizations. In Egypt, bees were revered as symbols of divine creation, their images adorning hieroglyphics and finding their way into religious ceremonies. The Greeks, captivated by the bees' intricate social structures and industrious nature, dedicated entire treatises to understanding their behavior. Even the pragmatic Romans, known for their engineering prowess, developed sophisticated hive designs and implemented laws to protect these valuable insects.

Beekeeping continued to flourish throughout the Middle Ages, fueled by advancements in hive technology. The widespread adoption of the Langstroth hive in the 19th century revolutionized the practice, making it more accessible and manageable for beekeepers of all levels.

Today, the story continues to evolve. From the adoption of beekeeping robots to the exploration of sustainable practices, we strive to ensure the well-being of these vital pollinators in the face of modern challenges like climate change and habitat loss. Understanding beekeeping history isn't just about appreciating the past; it's about recognizing the responsibility we inherit as modern beekeepers. We become stewards of a tradition that stretches back millennia, deeply intertwined with human history and the health of our planet. As you embark on your beekeeping journey, remember, you're not just tending to hives; you're connecting with a timeless story, one buzzing with wonder, significance, and a shared responsibility for the future.

Why are bees important for the ecosystem?

As beekeepers, we spend countless hours tending to our hives, carefully coaxing golden rewards from these remarkable creatures. But what we witness daily – the tireless work, the buzzing energy, the intricate social organization – are mere glimpses into the profound impact bees have on our world. Let's delve deeper and discover why these fuzzy architects are truly ecological game-changers, why caring for them is caring for our world, and how your decision to become a beekeeper is a step towards a brighter future.

Imagine a silent landscape, devoid of vibrant wildflowers, bursting fruits, and the chirping of birds. This stark reality paints a picture of a world without bees, highlighting their irreplaceable role in pollination. With each flit between blossoms, they act as nature's cupid, transferring pollen and enabling the reproduction of over 90% of flowering plants. This simple act sets in motion a ripple effect, nourishing food chains from the tiniest insects to the largest mammals. Fruits, vegetables, nuts, and seeds – the very foundation of our diet and countless ecosystems – owe their existence to these dedicated pollinators. Their absence would create a domino effect, disrupting food webs, decimating biodiversity, and ultimately threatening the very fabric of life on Earth.

Bees are not just ecological heroes; they also offer a powerful model for sustainable practices. Beekeepers often champion natural methods, creating healthy hives that hum with life. Planting bee-friendly flowers becomes not just an aesthetic choice, but a commitment to fostering biodiversity and providing crucial nectar sources. Responsible honey harvesting ensures the well-being of colonies, allowing them to thrive and continue their vital work. In essence, by becoming a beekeeper, you're not just producing a sweet treat; you're actively contributing to a future where human needs and ecological balance coexist in harmony.

The fate of bees and the fate of our planet are tightly interwoven. Declines in bee populations serve as a stark warning about the impact of climate change, habitat loss, and pesticide use. These tiny creatures are sensitive indicators of environmental health, and their struggles reflect the challenges facing our entire ecosystem. By choosing to become a beekeeper, you've taken a vital step towards environmental balance. You've become a steward of these vital pollinators, contributing to the health of local ecosystems, ensuring food security for future generations, and promoting biodiversity across the globe.

Your dedication ripples outwards, impacting not just your backyard hives but contributing to a global movement of bee champions working towards a healthier planet.

Understanding and protecting bees extends far beyond the present. These industrious insects hold the key to unlocking solutions for future challenges. Their efficient communication systems, complex social structures, and remarkable adaptations offer inspiration for advancements in technology, agriculture, and even medicine. Studying bees provides valuable insights into the delicate balance of nature, helping us develop sustainable practices for the future. By delving deeper into their world, we unlock not just fascinating biological secrets, but also the potential to build a world where humans and nature thrive in harmony.

Now, as we prepare to embark on a journey into the fascinating world of honeybee anatomy and physiology, remember that you're not just studying the workings of an insect. You're gaining knowledge about a vital cog in the machine of life, a creature whose well-being is intricately linked to our own. In the next section, we'll dissect the marvels of their bodies, from their complex communication systems to their intricate adaptations for efficient honey production.

Congratulations again on joining the ranks of beekeepers. Remember, you're not just managing hives; you're contributing to a global movement of bee champions, ensuring a vibrant and sustainable future for our planet, one buzz at a time.

Anatomy and physiology of a honeybee

Ever wondered what makes our fuzzy friends tick? From their tireless flight to their intricate comb designs, honeybees possess hidden wonders waiting to be explored. Lets peek beneath the exoskeleton and uncover some fascinating secrets around the main building blocks of a honeybee.

1. Building Blocks of a Bee:

- **Exoskeleton:** Imagine a suit of armor made of lightweight yet sturdy plates. That's the exoskeleton, providing bees with protection, support, and attachment points for muscles and legs.
- **Head:** Home to the compound eyes for multifaceted vision, antennae for sensing smells and tastes, and powerful mouthparts for collecting nectar and pollen.
- **Thorax:** The powerhouse of the bee, housing muscles that power their wings and legs, enabling them to navigate the world with impressive agility.
- **Abdomen:** Where magic happens! This segmented region houses the honey stomach, digestive system, sting apparatus, and wax glands, playing a vital role in honey production, communication, and defense.

2. Diving Deeper: Organ Systems

- **Circulatory System:** An open circulatory system transports hemolymph, delivering nutrients and removing waste throughout the bee's body.
- **Respiratory System:** Tracheae, a network of air tubes, provide oxygen directly to cells, allowing bees to maintain high energy levels during their tireless work.
- **Nervous System:** Complex and decentralized, enabling bees to respond to their environment, navigate efficiently, and communicate effectively within the hive.
- **Sensory Systems:** Beyond sight and smell, bees possess specialized receptors for detecting temperature, humidity, and even magnetic fields, guiding their remarkable navigational skills.

3. Specialized Adaptations:

- **Pollen Baskets:** Located on their hind legs, these hairy structures allow bees to efficiently collect and transport pollen back to the hive.
- **Honey Sac:** A specialized stomach where nectar is temporarily stored and undergoes enzymatic changes before becoming honey.

- **Wax Glands:** Located on the underside of the abdomen, these glands secrete wax used for building combs, storing honey, and communicating within the hive.

4. A Symphony of Organs:

While we've explored individual organs, remember that they function in perfect harmony. From the efficient breakdown of nectar to the precise construction of honeycomb, each system plays a crucial role in the bee's survival and the well-being of the entire colony.

By understanding the intricate anatomy and physiology of the honeybee, we gain a deeper appreciation for their remarkable capabilities and the challenges they face. This knowledge empowers us to become better beekeepers, providing optimal care and contributing to the health of these vital pollinators.

Colony structure and social behavior

Ever stand beside a buzzing beehive, mesmerized by the organized hum that fills the air? It might seem like pure chaos, but beneath the surface lies a world teeming with intricate social structures and remarkable behavior. For aspiring beekeepers, or anyone curious about these fascinating creatures, understanding this hidden world isn't just interesting, it's truly essential. By peeking into the heart of the hive, we unlock the secrets to caring for bees in a way that respects their natural rhythms and helps them thrive.

Imagine a bustling metropolis with clearly defined roles and a shared purpose. At the center sits the queen, the colony's heart, responsible for egg-laying and ensuring its future. Workers, the tireless backbone, form the majority, diligently performing diverse tasks like foraging, constructing comb, tending to brood, and defending the hive. Their roles even shift throughout their lives, showcasing remarkable adaptability. Drones, the males, have a singular purpose: mating with the queen to ensure genetic diversity. Despite their shorter lifespan, each bee plays a vital role in the symphony of the hive.

The hive buzzes with communication, but not just sound. The waggle dance, a bee's "language," is a captivating sight. Returning foragers perform this intricate dance, communicating the location and quality of a food source through the direction, duration, and intensity of their movements. This remarkable form of communication allows other bees to efficiently locate resources, maximizing foraging efficiency. But communication goes beyond dance. Pheromones, chemical signals undetectable to us, play a crucial role. An alarm pheromone alerts the hive to danger, while queen pheromones maintain social cohesion and regulate worker behavior. This invisible language forms the foundation of the colony's complex communication network.

Within the hive, chaos is kept at bay by various mechanisms. Queen dominance ensures reproductive control and social stability. Policing behavior by worker bees keeps everyone in line, preventing shirking and maintaining order. This intricate web of checks and balances allows the colony to function smoothly, ensuring the survival and well-being of all members.

Each bee may have a limited lifespan, but the colony endures. This seemingly paradoxical reality comes from the concept of the superorganism. Individual bees act as replaceable parts, working seamlessly towards a collective goal: the hive's survival. This unified behavior, often compared to the coordinated movements of a flock of birds, showcases the remarkable collective intelligence present within the hive.

Did you know bees can count, adjust their dances based on wind direction, and even mummify intruders within the hive? These fascinating examples highlight the intricate cognitive abilities and problem-solving skills present within bee colonies. Observing and understanding these behaviors not only fuels our sense of wonder but also deepens our appreciation for the remarkable creatures we care for.

Understanding colony structure and social behavior isn't just fascinating; it's essential for responsible beekeeping. By respecting the natural order of the hive, minimizing disruptions, and providing optimal conditions, we can ensure the well-being of our bees and encourage their flourishing. This includes practices like minimizing hive manipulations, providing ample forage opportunities, and utilizing bee-friendly equipment. By working in harmony with nature, we not only ensure the success of our bees but also contribute to the health of our entire ecosystem.

Remember, beekeeping is a journey of learning and wonder. As you observe your bees and understand their amazing social structure, you'll not only be a better beekeeper, but you'll also develop a deep respect for these incredible creatures. So, start exploring the fascinating world of the hive – you might be surprised at what you discover!

CHAPTER 2

GETTING THE RIGHT GEAR

Welcome to the exciting world of beekeeping equipment! While the bees themselves are undoubtedly the stars of the show, having the right tools at your disposal is crucial for ensuring their well-being, your safety, and ultimately, your enjoyment of this rewarding practice. This chapter equips you with the knowledge to confidently select, use, and care for your beekeeping gear, laying the foundation for a successful and safe apiary experience.

We'll delve into the essential equipment used by beekeepers, from hive components and frames to smoker and hive tools. You'll learn about the purpose of each piece and how to use it effectively for tasks like inspections, honey collection, and swarm control.

Safety is paramount in any beekeeping endeavor. We'll emphasize the importance of proper protective gear, including ventilated suits, veils, gloves, and boots. You'll learn about different suit materials, ventilation types, and how to choose the right gear for your needs and comfort. More importantly, we'll delve into crucial safety practices to minimize the risk of stings and ensure a calm and confident approach when working with your bees.

Finally, we'll cover the essential practice of maintaining and disinfecting your equipment. Learn about proper cleaning techniques, storage considerations, and the importance of hygiene in preventing the spread of disease within your apiary.

Remember, your beekeeping journey starts with the right gear. This chapter equips you with the knowledge and confidence to choose wisely, use responsibly, and care for your tools, ensuring a safe and successful beekeeping experience for both you and your buzzing friends.

Essential beekeeping equipment and its use

Before you delve into your apiary adventures, you'll need some essential gear to ensure both your safety and the well-being of your buzzing buddies. Don't worry, getting equipped doesn't require a royal ransom – we'll guide you through the must-haves and some helpful extras, keeping things beginner-friendly and budget-conscious.

Think of your beekeeping suit as your superhero armor! Look for a bee suit made of breathable yet protective material like cotton or canvas, with an attached veil and gloves. Remember, comfort is key – you'll be spending time in this suit, so choose one that allows for easy movement and ventilation. Consider your climate and preferences when selecting the veil style, opting for a full veil for maximum protection or a mesh veil for better visibility. Gloves should be thick enough to prevent stings but flexible enough for delicate tasks. Remember, bees can only sting through rough surfaces, so tuck your pants into your boots and secure any gaps to avoid unwelcome surprises.

Traditionally, beekeepers use smoke to calm bees during inspections. However, using smoke responsibly is crucial. If you choose to use a smoker, try to only use it sparingly to minimize stress on the bees. Consider alternative methods like using a bee brush or simply moving slowly and confidently to create a calmer environment.

Now that you're protected, let's explore the tools that help you interact with your hive effectively. Your trusty hive tool is a multi-purpose marvel, used for prying frames apart, scraping propolis (a bee resin), and gently nudging bees. Opt for a sturdy, well-balanced tool that fits comfortably in your hand. A frame lifter makes handling frames during inspections a breeze, reducing stress on both you and the bees. Remember, gentle movements are key to a happy hive! For brushing bees off frames before inspection, a soft-bristled brush is your friend. Queen excluders are optional tools that restrict the queen's movement between brood and honey chambers. While they can simplify honey harvesting, they can also disrupt natural colony dynamics. Consider your beekeeping goals and research their pros and cons before using them.

Extracting that golden goodness is a rewarding experience! For smaller operations, a manual extractor is a cost-effective option. If you have larger colonies or plan to harvest frequently, consider investing in an electric extractor. Remember, honey extraction requires specific equipment and techniques. Familiarize yourself with the process before diving in, and consider joining a beekeeping club or workshop for hands-on guidance.

Uncapping knives come in various styles, each with its own advantages. Heated knives make the process faster but require careful temperature control to avoid damaging the honey. Cold knives are safer for beginners but may take longer. Choose the style that best suits your comfort level and honey production goals. Finally, strainers and settling tanks help remove impurities and debris from your honey before processing. It's like giving your honey a spa treatment before bottling it up!

Just like any happy home needs regular check-ups, so does your hive! A hive thermometer helps you monitor internal temperature, crucial for optimal colony health. If you're managing larger apiaries, a hive scale can track colony weight changes, indicating honey production and resource needs.

Here is the summary of the essential beekeeping tools for beginners:

Protection:

- Bee suit with attached veil and gloves
- Boots

Hive Manipulation:

- Hive tool
- Frame lifter
- Soft-bristled brush
- (Optional) Queen excluder

Honey Extraction:

- (Optional) Extractor (manual or electric)
- (Optional) Smoker
- Uncapping knife
- Strainer
- Settling tank

Monitoring:

- Hive thermometer

Note: While some tools are marked optional, their necessity may depend on your specific goals and preferences.

Beekeeping is a rewarding adventure, but safety and responsibility come first. Choose high-quality, well-maintained equipment, and always handle your bees with respect and care. With the right gear and knowledge, you'll be well on your way to creating a thriving apiary and enjoying the many benefits of beekeeping.

Importance of protective gear and safety practices

While the thought of tending to your own buzzing brood might be exhilarating, remember, beekeeping involves interacting with creatures renowned for their potent sting. But fear not, new beekeeper! With the right knowledge and gear, you can ensure a safe and enjoyable experience for both you and your bees. Let's delve into the importance of protective gear and essential safety practices, transforming you from a nervous newbie to a confident, responsible beekeeper.

First things first: let's talk about stings. Most bee stings are localized reactions causing pain, redness, and swelling. They're generally unpleasant but manageable. However, a small percentage of people are allergic to bee venom, experiencing severe reactions that require immediate medical attention. Knowing your allergies is crucial. Consult your doctor before starting beekeeping, and always carry an EpiPen if necessary.

Remember that essential first line of defense we mentioned earlier – your bee suit? Think of it as your personal bee-fortress, keeping you shielded from potential stings while you navigate your busy apiary kingdom. It's crucial to choose one crafted from breathable materials like cotton or canvas, allowing you to move freely and stay cool under the warm sun. An attached veil and gloves are non-negotiable, of course, providing a complete barrier against those tiny stingers. When selecting your veil style, prioritize both comfort and protection. Opt for full coverage for maximum peace of mind, or choose a mesh veil for better visibility if you're feeling confident. Remember, tucking your pants into your boots and sealing any gaps is a beekeeper's secret weapon, ensuring those buzzing visitors stay on the outside where they belong!

While your suit acts as your fortress, a few additional tools can go a long way in fostering a calm and harmonious environment for both you and your bees. A hive tool becomes your trusty sidekick, helping you gently pry apart frames and nudge curious bees aside during inspections. Think of it as a multi-purpose beekeeping wand! A frame lifter elevates your frame handling game, making those delicate inspections smoother and easier on both you and your colony. And remember, gentle movements are key to keeping everyone happy. A soft-bristled brush becomes your secret weapon for gently coaxing bees off frames before inspection, minimizing stress and disruptions.

We mentioned smokers earlier as a traditional method for calming bees. While some beekeepers still use them, it's important to remember that smoke can be

14

stressful for bees. Responsible use is crucial, and alternative methods like using a bee brush or simply moving slowly and confidently can be just as effective in creating a calmer environment. Consider all your options and choose what feels most comfortable and responsible for you and your buzzing buddies.

Now that you're geared up, remember, respectful interactions are key to a harmonious apiary. Minimize disturbances to the hive by limiting inspections and avoiding loud noises or sudden movements. Use smoke sparingly if at all, opting for gentler methods. Remember, bees communicate through vibrations, so move slowly and deliberately around the hive to avoid startling them.

Accidents happen, even with the best gear and practices. Assemble a beekeeping-specific first-aid kit containing antihistamines, pain relievers, and sting soothers. Know how to treat common bee stings and recognize the signs of a severe allergic reaction. Always have an emergency plan in place, informing someone about your beekeeping activities and having their contact details readily available.

Bonus Tips for Beekeeping Bliss:

- Work with a partner, especially when starting out.
- Inform your neighbors about your beekeeping activities to foster understanding.
- Be aware of potential hazards in your apiary environment, like tripping hazards or poisonous plants.

By prioritizing safety and adopting responsible beekeeping practices, you'll create a thriving apiary where both you and your bees can buzz happily. Remember, knowledge is power – utilize online resources, beekeeping communities, and experienced mentors to continuously learn and refine your practices.

Maintaining and disinfecting equipment

Just like your trusty tools at home, your beekeeping equipment needs regular care and maintenance to ensure both its longevity and the well-being of your buzzing friends. Think of it as keeping your beekeeping arsenal in tip-top shape, ready for action whenever your apiary beckons! Let's delve into the essential practices of cleaning, disinfecting, and storing your gear, transforming you from a novice with a dusty hive tool to a seasoned pro with equipment that shines almost as brightly as your golden honey!.

Regular cleaning isn't just about keeping things tidy; it's crucial for your bees' health and ensures your equipment lasts for years to come. Imagine using dirty tools on your kitchen utensils – not ideal, right? The same applies to your beekeeping gear. Aim to clean your tools after every use, especially those that come into direct contact with bees and honey, like hive tools, frames, and extractors. For less frequently used items, monthly cleaning is sufficient.

Luckily, you don't need fancy concoctions to keep your beekeeping gear squeaky clean. Opt for simple, bee-friendly solutions like a mixture of warm water and dish soap, diluted bleach (wear gloves!), or even just plain water with a bit of elbow grease. Remember, harsh chemicals can harm your bees and contaminate your honey, so stick to natural solutions.

While regular cleaning keeps things hygienic, sometimes you need to go the extra mile. Disinfection is necessary when dealing with potential diseases or pest infestations to prevent their spread. Think of it as giving your equipment a deep clean with superpowers! Depending on the situation, you can opt for various methods like a bleach solution or steam cleaning. Always research the most suitable method for your specific situation and equipment, prioritizing the safety of your bees and yourself. Remember, proper disposal of cleaning solutions is essential to protect the environment.

Just like you wouldn't leave your favorite tools lying around in the rain, your beekeeping gear deserves proper storage. Find a cool, dry, and well-ventilated location away from direct sunlight and pests. Organize your equipment neatly, making it easy to find what you need and preventing damage from clutter. Tip: Hang frames vertically to prevent wax from warping, and store extractors with lids tightly closed to keep dust and debris at bay.

Some tools in your beekeeping arsenal require extra attention. Hive tools need regular sharpening to keep them effective. Smokers benefit from occasional chimney cleaning to ensure proper airflow. Extractors require thorough cleaning and sanitation after each use, paying special attention to nooks and crannies where honey might accumulate.

Even with the best care, your equipment might encounter some bumps along the way. Rust on hive tools? Soak them in vinegar or a rust remover solution. Wax buildup on frames? Heat them gently to melt the wax, scraping it off carefully. Remember, regular maintenance is key to preventing these issues and extending the lifespan of your beekeeping gear. Learn to recognize signs of wear and tear, like cracked frames or dull blades, and replace equipment when necessary.

By following these simple yet effective practices for maintaining and disinfecting your equipment, you'll ensure your beekeeping journey is filled with happy, healthy bees and sparkling tools – a true win-win! Remember, a little care and maintenance goes a long way in this fascinating world of beekeeping, so grab your cleaning supplies, roll up your sleeves, and get ready to keep your beekeeping arsenal buzzing with efficiency and care!

CHAPTER 3

SETTING UP YOUR HIVE

Ready to become a beekeeper? The thrill of witnessing your first bees buzzing into their new home awaits! But before the honey flows, Chapter 3 guides you through the exciting yet crucial step of setting up your hive. Buckle up, future beekeeper, as we unlock the secrets to creating a haven for your future honey-making friends.

First, we'll explore the fascinating world of hive types. Discover the pros and cons of popular options like Langstroth hives, top-bar hives, and Warre hives, helping you choose the perfect match for your location, bees, and beekeeping style. No more feeling overwhelmed by unfamiliar terms!

But choosing the right hive isn't enough. We'll delve into the intricacies of preparing your chosen hive for its tiny residents. Learn about essential components like frames, foundation, and hive tools, and master the art of assembling your hive with confidence. Think of it as building a tiny bee palace!

Now comes the exciting part: acquiring your bees! We'll guide you through the process of selecting a healthy swarm, whether you choose to capture a wild swarm or purchase bees from a reputable breeder. You'll learn how to identify healthy bees and ensure they transition smoothly into their new home.

This concise overview merely hints at the wealth of information packed into this chapter. You'll find detailed instructions and practical tips to ensure your beekeeping journey starts on the right foot. Remember, beekeeping is an enriching adventure, and this chapter equips you with the knowledge and confidence to make it a success!

Popular hive types for your location and needs

As you stand on the threshold of your beekeeping journey, selecting the right hive is a crucial decision. This section will be your guide through the diverse landscape of popular hive types, helping you understand their advantages and potential drawbacks. Forget wading through overwhelming technical jargon! We'll break down the most common options like Langstroth, Top-Bar, and Warre hives, highlighting their key features and how they impact your beekeeping experience.

Choosing a hive isn't just about finding the perfect bee apartment; it's about creating an optimal environment for both your buzzing residents and yourself! In this section, we'll move beyond the technical specifications and delve deeper into how your location and personal needs influence the ideal hive selection.

Remember, the "best" hive is not a singular answer. Climate, available space, honey production goals, and your comfort level all play a crucial role. Whether you're drawn to traditional options like the Langstroth or intrigued by alternative designs like the Warre, we'll explore how each responds to different environments and beekeeping styles.

Beginner beekeepers deserve a friendly introduction to the world of hives. We'll avoid delving into overly complex details, focusing on practical considerations and providing clear explanations. By the end of this section, you'll feel confident selecting a hive that sets you up for success and fosters a thriving bee colony, marking the exciting first step in your beekeeping adventure! Let's start with three most popular hive types.

1. The Classic Langstroth Hive: Tradition with a Twist and Adapting to Your Beekeeping World

Ah, the Langstroth hive! This beekeeping veteran boasts a rich history dating back to the 1850s. If you picture a beehive, chances are it's a Langstroth. Today, it's the most widely used hive globally, and for good reason: it's reliable, versatile, and relatively easy to work with.

Think of it like Lego for bees: The Langstroth is built with modular boxes stacked on top of each other, each housing removable frames for easy inspection and honey harvesting. Finding Langstroth equipment and replacement parts is a breeze, just like finding those colorful bricks! But before you dive in, let's tailor the Langstroth to your specific needs:

Demystifying the Climate:

- **Temperature:** Langstroth hives perform well in moderate climates, but extreme heat or cold can require additional insulation or ventilation adjustments. Consider your local temperatures and adjust accordingly.
- **Humidity:** High humidity can encourage mold growth within the hive. Ensure proper ventilation and consider hive placement in well-ventilated areas.
- **Wind:** Strong winds can topple hives. Secure your Langstroth with sturdy hive stands and windbreaks, especially in exposed locations.

Matching Your Space:

- **Size matters:** Langstroth hives come in various sizes, so choose one that fits your available yard space. Remember, beehives need space for bees to fly freely and for you to access them comfortably.
- **Stacking it up:** The modular design allows you to add boxes as your colony grows, but keep in mind the weight of honey-filled boxes and your ability to lift them safely.

Aligning Your Goals:

- **Honey enthusiast?** Langstroth hives are efficient honey producers, thanks to their easily removable frames. However, if maximizing honey production is your top priority, explore other options like double brood Langstroths.
- **Natural beekeeping advocate?** While Langstroth offers bee-friendly features, some find its frame system limits natural comb building. Consider alternative hives like Warre or Top-Bar if this resonates more with you.

Prioritizing Your Comfort:

- **Lifting and manipulating:** Langstroth hives can get heavy, especially with honey. Consider your physical abilities and enlist help if needed. Alternatively, explore lighter hive options like Warre.
- **Management intensity:** Langstroth requires regular inspections and manipulations. If you prefer a more hands-off approach, consider Top-Bar hives or those with less frequent intervention needs.

Choosing a hive is a personal decision, and the Langstroth is a solid choice for beginners thanks to its ease of use and widespread support.

2. The Top-Bar Hive: Embrace Natural Harmony and Bee-Centric Care

Step away from the traditional and delve into the world of the Top-Bar hive, a philosophy grounded in simplicity and respecting the bees' natural instincts. Imagine a rustic, horizontal sanctuary, where bees sculpt intricate comb patterns on long bars instead of individual frames. Think of it as a minimalist bee apartment, prioritizing bee well-being and minimal intervention.

Unlike its boxy counterpart, the Top-Bar hive exudes a natural charm, resembling a bee-crafted chalet nestled in your backyard. But don't mistake its simplicity for lack of depth – this hive pulsates with the rhythm of the bees themselves, offering a unique beekeeping experience that prioritizes observation and respect for their natural ways.

So, before you embark on your Top-Bar journey, let's explore how this hive adapts to your specific location, needs, and beekeeping vision:

Demystifying the Climate:

- **Temperature:** Top-Bar hives perform well in mild to warm climates. Extreme heat might require additional shade or ventilation adjustments, while cold winters necessitate proper insulation. Research your local climate and adapt accordingly.
- **Humidity:** Similar to Langstroths, high humidity can encourage mold growth. Ensure proper ventilation and consider hive placement in well-ventilated areas. Top-Bar hives with open designs might naturally promote better airflow.
- **Wind:** While generally stable, strong winds can affect Top-Bar hives due to their horizontal layout. Secure your hive with sturdy stands and windbreaks, especially in exposed locations.

Matching Your Space:

- **Size matters:** Top-Bar hives come in various lengths, so choose one that fits your available yard space. Remember, bees need flight space and you need access for inspections and harvesting.

- **Horizontal Harmony:** Unlike Langstroths, Top-Bar hives don't stack vertically. Consider the available ground space and potential future expansion needs when choosing the length.

Aligning Your Goals:

- **Honey enthusiast?** While possible, Top-Bar hives generally produce lower honey yields compared to Langstroths. If maximizing honey production is your top priority, explore other options like double brood Langstroths.
- **Natural beekeeping advocate?** This is where Top-Bar shines! Bees build natural comb freely, fostering their natural behavior and potentially improving honey quality. If this resonates with you, Top-Bar delivers true bee-centricity.

Prioritizing Your Comfort:

- **Lifting and manipulation:** Top-Bar hives are generally lighter than Langstroths, especially if managed with shorter bars. However, lifting full honey bars can still require some muscle. Consider your physical abilities and adjust bar length accordingly.
- **Management intensity:** Top-Bar requires less frequent inspections and manipulations compared to Langstroths, aligning with its hands-off philosophy. However, learning new techniques and adapting to natural comb management is crucial.

Remember, the "best" hive depends on your priorities and preferences. The top-bar hive offers a unique bee-centric experience, perfect for those drawn to natural beekeeping and comfortable with a slightly different approach.

3. Unveiling the Bee-Centric Haven: Exploring the Warre Hive

Step aside from the conventional and enter the realm of the Warre hive, a philosophy rooted in harmony with nature and minimal intervention. Imagine a charming, square-shaped bee abode, built with thin boxes stacked like rustic pancakes. Inside, bees construct natural comb on wide bars, fostering a bee-centric environment that echoes their innate instincts.

Think of it as a bee spa, prioritizing the bees' well-being above all else. Warre hives minimize manipulations, allowing you to observe rather than manipulate, and honey harvesting involves removing entire boxes (honeycomb and all!), reducing stress on the colony.

But before you don your beekeeping hat and approach this natural haven, let's tailor the Warre hive to your specific location, needs, and beekeeping vision:

Understanding the Climate:

- **Temperature:** Warre hives perform well in moderate climates. Extreme temperatures might require additional insulation or ventilation adjustments for optimal bee comfort.
- **Humidity:** Similar to Langstroth and Top-Bar hives, high humidity can encourage mold growth. Ensure proper ventilation and consider placement in well-ventilated areas.
- **Wind:** Secure your hive with sturdy stands and windbreaks, especially in exposed locations, as the stacked box design can be susceptible to strong winds.

Matching Your Space:

- **Size matters:** Warre hives are often smaller than Langstroths, making them ideal for smaller yards or beekeepers seeking a hands-off approach. They're easier to lift and manage, especially for beginners.
- **Stacking Simplicity:** Unlike Langstroths, Warre hives have a limited stacking capacity due to their weight. Consider your space limitations and potential honey production goals when choosing the number of boxes.

Aligning Your Goals:

- **Honey enthusiast?** While Warre bees produce delicious honey, the overall yield is generally lower compared to Langstroths. If maximizing honey production is your top priority, this might not be the best choice.
- **Natural beekeeping advocate?** This is where the Warre hive truly shines! Less intervention fosters natural comb building and bee behavior, potentially improving honey quality and colony health.

Prioritizing Your Comfort:

- **Lifting and manipulation:** Warre hives are generally lighter than Langstroths, especially with fewer boxes. However, even single boxes can be heavy when full of honey. Consider your physical abilities and lifting assistance if needed.
- **Management intensity:** Warre requires less frequent inspections and manipulations compared to Langstroths, aligning with its hands-off philosophy. However, adapting to natural comb management and understanding bee behavior are crucial.

If you're drawn to a natural, bee-centric approach and the idea of minimal intervention appeals to you, the Warre hive could be your perfect match. Just remember, knowledge and adaptation are key!

4. Beyond the Big Three: Exploring Alternative Hive Options

Langstroth and Warre may be the reigning champions, but the world of beekeeping offers a wealth of fascinating alternatives! Let's peek beyond the big three and explore some truly unique hive options:

- **Kenyan Top-Bar Hive:** This bee-friendly design hails from Africa, featuring long, sloping bars where bees build natural comb. Imagine a rustic bee chalet, perfect for hands-off beekeepers who prioritize natural processes. However, honey harvesting requires removing entire bars, and finding resources might be trickier.
- **Flow Hive:** Ever dreamed of harvesting honey straight from the tap? The Flow Hive boasts a built-in system that allows you to extract

honey without disturbing the bees or their brood. Sounds magical, right? But remember, some beekeepers raise concerns about its impact on bee behavior and honey quality. Do your research before diving in!

- **Warre Flow Hive:** Combining the Warre philosophy with Flow Hive technology, this option offers natural comb building with the convenience of tappable honey. However, it inherits the limitations of both parent designs, requiring specific knowledge and potentially lower honey yields.

4. Other Buzz-Worthy Options: The beekeeping world is vast! Briefly consider:

- **Bush Beehive:** Traditionally woven from natural materials, these African hives promote natural beekeeping and are perfect for experienced beekeepers seeking a cultural immersion.
- **Beehaus:** Think charming bee cottages! These European-inspired hives prioritize aesthetics and minimal intervention, but require advanced knowledge and are better suited for smaller bee populations.

5. My Top Pick for Beginner Beekeepers: A Hive for Success

Remember, choosing a hive is a personal journey. Choosing the "best" beginner hive is tricky, as every beekeeper and their apiary have unique needs. However, I can offer my recommendation based on my experience and the common challenges first-timers face:

For me, the top choice for beginner beekeepers is the Langstroth hive. Why?

- **Accessibility:** Langstroth equipment is widely available, so finding replacement parts and resources is a breeze. This makes troubleshooting and learning easier, especially for new beekeepers navigating an unfamiliar world.
- **Standardized Frames:** Removable frames simplify inspections and honey harvesting, crucial for new beekeepers unfamiliar with bee

behavior. Their standardized size means you can swap them around, add more boxes as your colony grows, and find replacement frames with ease.

- **Versatility:** The modular design allows you to adjust the hive size by adding boxes, catering to your colony's growth and honey production goals. This avoids the need to switch hives later, saving you time and resources.
- **Climate considerations:** While Langstroths perform well in moderate climates, extreme temperatures might require additional insulation or ventilation adjustments. Research your local climate and adjust accordingly. Remember, proper hive placement and wind protection are crucial for any hive type.
- **Space matters:** Langstroth hives come in various sizes, so choose one that fits your available yard space. Remember, bees need flight space, and you need access for inspections and harvesting. The modular design lets you expand vertically, but keep the weight of honey-filled boxes in mind.
- **Honey production goals:** Langstroths are efficient honey producers thanks to their easily removable frames. However, if maximizing honey production is your top priority, explore double brood Langstroths or other options like Kenyan Top Bar hives.
- **Comfort level:** Lifting Langstroth hives, especially full of honey, can be challenging. Consider your physical abilities and enlist help if needed. While Langstroths require regular inspections and manipulations, they offer a good balance for beginners seeking a moderate level of intervention.

Ultimately, the "best" hive is the one that resonates with your learning style, preferences, and resources. If you're drawn to natural beekeeping methods, research alternative options like Warre or Top-Bar hives carefully. But if you prioritize ease of use and readily available support, the Langstroth hive is a fantastic starting point for your beekeeping adventure!

Assembling and preparing your hive for bees

The moment your hive arrives is buzzing with excitement! Now it's time to transform this wooden box into a welcoming haven for your future bee residents. Whether you've chosen a classic Langstroth, rustic Top-Bar, or charming Warre hive, let's guide you through the essential steps for assembly and preparation – with a focus on safe handling throughout the process.

1. Unboxing and Inspecting Your Hive

- **Get Acquainted:** With a sense of wonder, unpack your hive, carefully laying out each component. Familiarize yourself with the different parts – brood boxes, honey supers, inner cover, hive stand, etc. – and their roles in beekeeping life.
- **Quality Check:** Examine each piece for any damage, cracks, or warping. Ensure all necessary parts are present according to your specific hive model. Don't hesitate to contact your supplier if you encounter any issues.

2. Assembling Your Hive

- **Follow the Blueprint:** Each hive type has its unique assembly instructions. Consult the provided manual or online resources specific to your model. Lay out the components in the recommended order, and carefully follow the step-by-step guide.
- **Secure Connections:** Pay close attention to how components fit together. Ensure all connections are secure and properly aligned. Check for gaps or wobbly joints that could compromise the hive's integrity or invite unwanted guests.
- **Treatment Time (Optional):** Depending on your hive material and local climate, some beekeepers opt for applying treatments like wood stain or beeswax polish for added protection and longevity. Research best practices for your specific hive type and climate before proceeding.

3. Preparing Hive Components

Langstroth Hive:

- **Foundational Frames:** Equip your frames with foundation (pre-made beeswax sheets) or starter strips to encourage natural comb building. Follow instructions for proper installation and spacing.
- **Hive Entrance:** Depending on your colony size and season, install the appropriate entrance reducer to regulate bee traffic and maintain optimal hive temperature.

Top-Bar Hive:

- **Natural Canvas:** In a Top-Bar hive, bees build their own comb freely on long wooden bars. These bars should be securely attached within the hive but remain removable for inspections and honey harvesting.
- **Ventilation Matters:** Ensure proper ventilation with mesh screens placed strategically throughout the hive, allowing for airflow and preventing moisture buildup.

Warre Hive:

- **Honey Holes (Optional):** Warre hives typically have pre-drilled holes in the upper boxes for honey harvesting. If your model doesn't, follow recommended methods for creating them while ensuring structural integrity.
- **Natural Building Blocks:** Similar to Top-Bar hives, bees construct their comb on removable bars provided within the hive. Secure them properly for easy access during inspections.

4. Adding Extras

- **Sweet Options:** If desired, install a pollen trap or honey super (additional box for honey storage) based on your hive type and beekeeping goals. Adding a honey super allows you to harvest some of the bees' surplus without harming the colony. However, prioritize the bees' needs first. Wait until your colony is established and has filled most of the brood boxes before adding a super. Consult your specific hive type's guidelines for adding honey supers at the appropriate time.

- ○ **Langstroth Hives:** Use medium or shallow supers depending on your preference and honey flow. Add them above the brood boxes when at least 80% of frames are capped with honey.
- ○ **Top-Bar Hives:** Add empty bars to the back of the existing bars as needed. Harvest frames once fully drawn and capped with honey.
- ○ **Warre Hives:** Add honey boxes above the brood boxes when the top brood box is nearly full.

- **Level and Steady:** Place your hive on a sturdy, level stand made of concrete blocks, treated wood, or metal. Ensure it's stable and won't wobble or tip over in wind or weather. Leveling is crucial. Use a spirit level to check and adjust the stand if needed. An uneven hive can cause stress for the bees and make inspections difficult.

- **Feeding Time:** Prepare feeders and water sources near the hive entrance, keeping them readily accessible for your arriving bees. Bees need constant access to clean, fresh water. Place a shallow dish or bee-specific waterer filled with water near the hive entrance, ideally in a shaded area. Refresh the water regularly and clean the container to prevent disease. Also, If bees lack natural food sources early in spring or after a dearth (period with limited nectar and pollen), provide a sugar syrup feeder filled with a 1:1 ratio of white sugar and water. Ensure the feeder is bee-safe and doesn't allow drowning. Remove feeders once natural food sources become abundant.

5. Final Touches: Ensuring Your Hive is Bee-Ready

- **Pre-Cleaning:** Before welcoming your bees, give your hive a thorough cleaning. Use natural, bee-safe disinfectants or a light bleach solution (followed by thorough rinsing and drying) to remove any dust, debris, or potential contaminants.
- **Ventilation Check:** Double-check that your ventilation screens are secure and functioning properly. Adequate airflow is crucial for preventing moisture buildup and ensuring a healthy hive environment.

- **Entrance Adjustments:** Depending on your chosen hive type and the season, adjust the entrance reducer to the appropriate size to regulate bee traffic and maintain optimal hive temperature.
- **Initial Setup**: Arrange the hive components according to your preferred setup, keeping bee behavior and ease of access in mind. Consider factors like space for frames/bars, feeder placement, and future expansion needs.

Personalize It (Optional): Add a splash of personality by painting your hive (using bee-safe paint) or attaching identification markers for easy recognition in your apiary.

6. Tips for Handling Hive Components Safely

- **Wear protective gear**: Always wear beekeeping clothing including a veil, gloves, and long sleeves and pants when handling hive components, even during assembly. This protects you from stings and potential allergic reactions.
- **Lift with care:** Some hive parts, especially full honey supers, can be heavy. Use proper lifting techniques and enlist help if needed to avoid injury.
- **Inspect for hidden bees:** Before handling any component, especially used equipment, gently tap it and check for bees hiding in crevices or folds. Use a smoker if necessary to calm them down before proceeding.
- **Avoid rough handling:** Be mindful of delicate components like frames and mesh screens. Handle them with care to prevent damage and potential injury.
- **Store components safely:** When not in use, store hive components in a dry, well-ventilated location away from direct sunlight and potential pests. This helps maintain their lifespan and prevents damage.

Remember: This guide provides a general overview. Always consult specific instructions for your chosen hive model and adjust your approach based on your local climate and beekeeping goals. Always prioritize the bees' needs over maximizing honey production. Observe your bees and adjust your approach as needed to ensure their health and well-being.

Sourcing a healthy swarm of bees

The day your beekeeping journey truly begins isn't just about assembling hive parts – it's about welcoming the buzzing residents themselves! Sourcing a healthy swarm is an exciting, yet critical, first step. Choosing responsibly ensures a smooth transition for your new colony and sets the stage for a thriving apiary.

The sight of a swirling bee cloud is both awe-inspiring and a little chaotic. But this phenomenon, known as swarming, is actually a vital part of honeybee reproduction! Let's delve deeper into the fascinating world of swarms and help you navigate your search for buzzing buddies.

When a bee colony thrives, it eventually becomes too crowded. As a solution, the queen bee and a large portion of the worker bees embark on a journey to establish a new home. This "swarm" typically consists of 10,000 to 30,000 bees, buzzing together in a mesmerizing cloud.

While swarming can occur throughout the year in warmer climates, it usually happens during specific windows of opportunity. Knowing your region's swarming season is crucial for being prepared:

- North America: In the United States, swarming typically occurs between April and June, peaking in May. However, this can vary depending on your location. In Canada, expect swarms from late May to July.
- Europe: Swarms tend to happen between May and July, with warmer southern regions experiencing earlier activity.
- Africa and Australia: Due to their diverse climates, these regions have more varied swarming seasons. Research specifically for your local area.

Now, the exciting part – attracting these buzzing bundles of joy to your apiary! But remember, responsible sourcing is key. Here's how:

- **Beekeeping Groups:** Join local beekeeping clubs or online forums. Beekeepers often announce available swarms within their communities.
- **Swarm Removal Services:** Certified professionals help remove unwanted swarms humanely and responsibly. Many offer the option to rehome the swarm with an interested beekeeper.
- **Backyard Beekeepers:** Don't underestimate the power of your neighborhood! Ask around – there might be a beekeeper nearby with a swarm looking for a new home.

Remember, responsible sourcing starts with understanding the natural phenomenon of swarming and respecting the bees' welfare. By connecting with your local beekeeping community and utilizing available resources, you can find your perfect swarm and embark on a rewarding beekeeping journey!

2. Beyond the Swarm: Exploring Alternative Bee Acquisition Options

While sourcing a swarm offers a unique and exciting connection to the natural world of beekeeping, it's not the only way to welcome buzzing buddies into your apiary. Let's explore other popular options, each with its own set of pros and cons, to help you find the best fit for your goals and experience.

Established Nuclei:

- **What are they?** Nuclei are miniature colonies, typically housed in a small hive box with 5-10 frames containing brood (developing bees), adult bees, a queen, and honey and pollen stores. They're essentially "starter colonies" ready to grow and expand in your hive.
- **Purchasing**: Nuclei can be purchased from beekeepers, beekeeping supply companies, or online retailers. Look for reputable sources with experience in raising healthy bees.

- **Transportation:** Nuclei are usually transported in specially designed boxes with ventilation and food sources. Ensure proper temperature control and minimize travel time to minimize stress on the bees.
- **Pros:**
    - **Faster colony growth:** Nuclei already have a queen and brood, allowing for quicker honey production and colony expansion compared to packages.
    - **Less risk of absconding:** Established colonies with a queen are less likely to leave their new home compared to newly introduced packages.
    - **Less experience needed:** Nuclei require less hands-on care initially, making them suitable for beginner beekeepers.
- **Cons:**
    - **Higher cost:** Nuclei are generally more expensive than packages.
    - **Limited availability:** Availability may be seasonal or dependent on the supplier.
    - **Potential health concerns:** It's crucial to choose a reputable source with healthy colonies to avoid disease transmission.

Packages of Bees:

- **What are they?** Packages contain 3-4 pounds of live bees, including worker bees, a caged queen, and sometimes some attendants. They're essentially the "building blocks" for a new colony.
- **Purchasing:** Packages are readily available from beekeeping supply companies and online retailers. Choose reputable sources with good breeding practices and disease control measures.
- **Transportation:** Packages are typically shipped in ventilated cages with food sources. Ensure proper temperature control and minimize travel time to ensure bee health.
- **Pros:**
    - **Lower cost:** Packages are generally more affordable than nuclei.
    - **Wider availability:** Packages are often available year-round, offering more flexibility.

○ **Genetic selection:** You may have more choice in selecting specific bee breeds or desirable traits.

● **Cons:**

○ **Slower colony growth:** It takes longer for packages to establish a functioning colony and produce honey compared to nuclei.

○ **Higher risk of absconding:** Newly introduced packages without established brood are more likely to leave the hive if not managed properly.

○ **Requires more experience:** Managing package bees requires more hands-on care and knowledge to ensure their survival and successful integration.

Online Ordering:

While convenient, ordering bees online comes with additional considerations:

● **Reputable Source:** Thoroughly research the online vendor's reputation, breeding practices, and bee health guarantees before placing an order.

● **Shipping Logistics:** Ensure the vendor uses proper shipping methods with temperature control and guarantees live arrival.

● **Climate Considerations:** Choose bees suited to your local climate and nectar flow patterns for optimal colony success.

Selecting the right bees for your needs and experience level is crucial for a successful beekeeping journey. Consider your resources, time commitment, and desired outcomes when making your decision. Consulting experienced beekeepers or local beekeeping associations can also offer valuable guidance!

3. Sourcing the Right Bees for Your Region

Choosing the right honey bee breed for your location is like pairing the perfect dance partner – it ensures harmony and success! Let's explore honeybee breeds and their suitability for different US regions, considering climate, nectar flow, and temperament.

Northeast:

- **Climate:** Short warm season, diverse flora.
- **Nectar Flow:** Varied, with early spring blooms followed by summer abundance.
- **Temperament:** Consider your preference!
    - **Calm & productive:** Italians, Caucasians, or New World Carniolans offer a good balance.
    - **Excellent pollinators:** Buckfast bees are known for their vigor and pollen-collecting prowess.

Southeast:

- **Climate:** Humid, with long nectar flow.
- **Nectar Flow:** Abundant throughout most of the year.
- **Temperament:** Gentleness might be preferred due to warmer weather activity.
    - **Popular choices:** Italians are highly adaptable and productive. Gentler options include New World Carniolans or Buckfast bees.

Midwest:

- **Climate:** Varied, with hot summers, cold winters, and diverse nectar flow patterns.
- **Nectar Flow:** Short but intense in many areas.
- **Temperament:** Hardiness and adaptability are key.
    - **Consider:** Caucasians or hybrids are known for their resilience and good honey production.

Great Plains:

- **Climate:** Hot summers, cold winters, and limited nectar flow.
- **Nectar Flow:** Short and concentrated in specific periods.
- **Temperament:** Drought tolerance and efficient foraging are crucial.

- ○ **Options:** Caucasians and some hybrid bees are well-suited to these challenging conditions.

Southwest:

- **Climate:** Hot, dry climate with sparse floral resources.
- **Nectar Flow:** Limited and often unpredictable.
- **Temperament:** Africanized bees (with proper caution) or well-adapted hybrids might be suitable.
    - ○ **Important note:** Due to their defensive nature, Africanized bees are not recommended for beginners. Consider experienced beekeepers or specific hybrid strains with proper management.

Intermountain West:

- **Climate:** Diverse climates and flora.
- **Nectar Flow:** Varies depending on location and elevation.
- **Temperament:** Adaptability and good foraging skills are important.
    - ○ **Options:** Italians, Caucasians, or even Carniolan bees can perform well in these diverse regions.

Pacific Coast:

- **Climate:** Mediterranean climate with long nectar flow in many areas.
- **Nectar Flow:** Abundant and diverse in many regions.
- **Temperament:** Consider your preference and experience level.
    - ○ **Popular choices:** Italians are widely used for their productivity and ease of management. For gentler options, explore New World Carniolans or Buckfast bees.

This is just a starting point! Always consider your specific location, apiary setup, and personal preferences when selecting bees. Consulting with local beekeepers and beekeeping associations can provide invaluable insights into breeds that thrive in your area.

Additional Tips:

- **Start small:** If you're a beginner, consider starting with a smaller colony (nuclei) or package of bees to gain experience before expanding.
- **Research breeder practices:** Choose beekeepers who prioritize bee health, responsible breeding practices, and transparency.
- **Queen quality matters:** Ensure you receive a healthy, young queen with good genetics for optimal colony success.

By carefully considering your local climate, nectar flow, and desired temperament, you can choose the perfect honey bee breed for your apiary, setting the stage for a rewarding and harmonious beekeeping journey!

4. Beyond the Buzz: Assessing Swarm Health

Finding a swarm is exciting, but before you get swept away by the buzzing enthusiasm, it's crucial to assess their health. Remember, you're welcoming living creatures into your care, and their well-being should be your top priority. Imagine you're interviewing potential roommates. Here's what to observe in the swarm:

- **Energy Levels:** Are they a vibrant, cohesive bunch moving with purpose? A sluggish, listless swarm could indicate underlying issues.
- **Worker Power:** Look for a healthy ratio of worker bees, the colony's backbone. Too many drones (male bees) could suggest imbalance.
- **Brood Bliss:** The presence of brood (developing bees) signifies a healthy, reproducing colony. Look for capped brood cells, a sign of active development.
- **Alertness Matters:** Do the bees react swiftly to stimuli? Excessive calmness or disorientation could point to health problems.

Not all swarms are created equal. Be mindful of these potential warning signs:

- **Lethargy Lounge:** Bees moving slowly, with drooping wings or dragging abdomens, could indicate illness or weakness.
- **Deformed Dance:** Misshapen wings, unusual body parts, or abnormal sizes might suggest genetic issues or diseases.
- **Aggression Overload:** While some defensiveness is natural, excessive aggression could indicate stress, disease, or poor queen health.

Don't hesitate to express your concerns to the source. Responsible beekeepers welcome inquiries and should be transparent about any health checks or disease screenings conducted. If something feels off, trust your instincts and seek information from other beekeepers or beekeeping resources.

Choosing a healthy swarm sets the stage for a thriving colony and a rewarding beekeeping experience. Don't be afraid to walk away if you have doubts. By being a responsible and observant beekeeper, you'll ensure the well-being of your new buzzing buddies and lay the foundation for a harmonious future together!

5. Asking the Right Questions: Before You Buzz with Excitement!

Finding the perfect swarm is like meeting your dream roommate – you want someone compatible, healthy, and who fits your lifestyle. So before you get swept away by the buzzing enthusiasm, ask these key questions to ensure a smooth transition and a happy hive.

Don't be shy! Just like you'd ask about a pet's health, inquire about the swarm's recent health checks and disease screenings. Responsible beekeepers prioritize colony health and are happy to share:

- **Recent checkups:** When was the last health inspection? Were there any concerns identified?
- **Disease screenings:** Have they been tested for common bee diseases like American Foulbrood or European Foulbrood?

- **Treatment history:** Have they received any medications or treatments? If so, understand the potential impact on your new colony.

Bees come in all shapes and sizes (okay, mostly sizes), each with unique characteristics. Consider your hive type and desired bee traits:

- **Hive type:** Langstroth hives might prefer bees with calmer temperaments, while Top-Bar hives may be suitable for more active breeds.
- **Honey production:** Are you looking for high honey yields or bees known for their gentle nature?
- **Gentleness:** If you're a beginner or have concerns about stings, prioritize calm and docile bees.

Knowing the swarm's potential genetic background helps you anticipate their behavior and suitability for your specific needs. Ask about the source of the swarm, their breeding practices, and any known genetic traits.

Beekeeping regulations vary by location. Don't let excitement cloud your judgment! Before welcoming your buzzing buddies, understand:

- **Local regulations:** Are there any permits or registrations required for owning bees? Are there restrictions on swarm acquisition?
- **Required paperwork:** Does the source have any health certificates or documentation you need to obtain?
- **Bee transport regulations:** If transporting the swarm yourself, are there any specific guidelines or restrictions to follow?

Remember, responsible beekeeping starts with following the rules! By clarifying these legal aspects beforehand, you can avoid any future headaches and ensure a smooth start to your beekeeping journey.

6. A Gentle Introduction: Building Trust from the Start

So you've found the perfect swarm, healthy and compatible with your vision. Now comes the exciting, yet delicate, part: introducing them to their new home. Remember, these bees have just embarked on a major adventure, leaving their familiar world behind. Patience and respect are key to building trust and ensuring a smooth transition.

Imagine moving into a new house – everything is unfamiliar, maybe a bit overwhelming. The same goes for your bees! Don't rush the process:

- **Staged Arrival:** Consider "soft-releasing" the bees by gently placing the container near the hive entrance for a few hours, allowing them to explore their surroundings gradually.
- **Hive Preparation:** Ensure their new home is ready: clean, well-ventilated, with frames or foundation installed, and feeders filled with sugar water. Think of it as preparing a welcoming haven!
- **Follow the Hive Type Guide:** Different hive types have specific recommended introduction methods. Research the best approach for your setup to minimize stress and confusion.

Think of yourself as the friendly neighbor introducing yourself to newcomers. Here's how to cultivate a positive relationship:

- **Gentle Inspections:** Start with brief, calm observations, avoiding loud noises or sudden movements. Let them get used to your presence.
- **Minimal Disturbances:** Resist the urge to constantly peek and poke. Give them space to settle in and establish their routines.
- **Positive Interactions:** Offer sugar water outside the hive to create positive associations with your approach. Gradually, they'll learn to see you as a source of nourishment, not a threat.
- **Patience is Key:** Remember, building trust takes time. Be patient, respectful, and consistent in your interactions. Soon, those initial buzzes of uncertainty will turn into welcoming greetings!

Bonus Tip: Communication is key, even with bees! Talk softly and calmly while working around the hive. They may not understand the words, but they can pick up on the tone and intention.

By following these steps and prioritizing a gentle introduction, you'll lay the foundation for a harmonious relationship with your bees. Remember, they're not just fascinating creatures; they're your partners in this beekeeping adventure! Treat them with respect and care, and they'll reward you with years of buzzing joy and pollination magic.

Placing Bees in the Prepared Hive: A Beginner's Guide

The anticipation has been growing – you've meticulously crafted your hive, sourced your bees, and now it's time for the grand culmination: introducing your buzzing buddies to their new home! This moment marks the exciting transition from beekeeping theory to practice, the beginning of a beautiful partnership between you and your honey-producing friends. But don't buzz into this step just yet! A successful introduction requires careful planning, gentle handling, and a healthy dose of bee-lieve. Let's delve into the process, ensuring your bees feel welcome, settled, and ready to thrive in their new haven.

Think of this as planning the perfect housewarming party for your bees. You wouldn't want to throw it during a blizzard, right? Here are key factors to consider when choosing the ideal introduction day:

- **Weather:** Aim for a mild, sunny day with light winds. Extreme temperatures (hot or cold) or heavy rain can stress the bees and make acclimatization difficult. Early morning or late afternoon, when bee activity is naturally lower, is often preferable.
- **Season:** If possible, introduce your bees early in the spring when nectar flow is starting and the colony is naturally expanding. This gives them ample time to build comb, raise brood, and store honey before winter.

41

- **Local Expertise:** Consult your local beekeeping association or experienced beekeepers for region-specific recommendations. They can advise on optimal timing based on your climate and typical nectar flow patterns.

Sunshine signals a welcoming environment, but remember bees are sensitive to extremes. Don't place your hive in direct midday sun. Opt for dappled sunlight or partial shade, allowing them to regulate hive temperature efficiently. If the weather unexpectedly turns harsh, postpone the introduction and choose a more suitable day.

Suddenly dumping the bees into their new digs might seem efficient, but it can be stressful and confusing for them. Instead, offer a gradual introduction to minimize stress and promote a smooth transition. Here are two common methods:

Direct Release (Package Bees):

- Gently shake the package onto a screened bottom board with an empty hive body above. This allows them to acclimate to the hive environment gradually before exploring the frames.
- Minimize shaking time to avoid injuring the bees.
- Offer sugar water in a feeder outside the hive for immediate nourishment.
- Leave them undisturbed for several hours to explore and settle in.

Newspaper Method (Nuclei or Packages):

- Securely place the queen cage within the hive, ideally near the center of a brood frame.
- Cover the top of the frames with moistened newspaper and punch small holes.
- Allow worker bees to gradually chew their way through the newspaper and release the queen, mimicking a more natural emergence process.

- This method can take several hours or even a day. Be patient and avoid disturbing the bees while they work.

Additional Tips:

- **Choose the right method:** Consider your experience level, bee type, and weather conditions when deciding between direct release or the newspaper method.
- **Hydration is key:** Ensure the bees have access to fresh water, either through feeders or a nearby water source, throughout the acclimatization process.
- **Minimize stress:** Avoid loud noises, strong smells, or excessive hive manipulations during this delicate phase.
- **Observe their behavior:** Watch for signs of calmness, exploration, and interaction with the queen – these indicate a successful introduction.

Patience and respect are key when welcoming your new buzzing friends. By following these guidelines and prioritizing their well-being, you'll lay the foundation for a harmonious and rewarding beekeeping journey!

Remember the meticulous preparations we discussed in the previous sections? Now it's time to put the finishing touches on your buzzing kingdom, ensuring it's fit for royalty (of the buzzing variety)! Think of it as a final inspection before welcoming your long-awaited guests. Imagine moving into a new house with missing furniture and no food in the pantry – not ideal, right? Here's what your bees need for a comfortable arrival:

- **Frames:** Recall the importance of providing empty frames or wax foundation. These give your bees a base for building comb, their crucial home for raising brood and storing honey. Choose the type and number based on your hive type and goals.
- **Food:** Remember the sugar water feeders outside the hive? They remain vital, offering immediate nourishment and establishing a positive association with your presence. Consider pollen substitutes during low pollen periods (as mentioned previously).

- **Hive Entrance:** Don't forget the entrance reducer! Adjust it to an appropriate size for airflow control, pest prevention, and temperature regulation.
- **Temperature and Ventilation:** Proper ventilation through screened bottom boards and mesh openings is crucial. Avoid drafts and direct sunlight on the entrance, aiming for comfortable internal temperatures around 95°F.
- **Cleanliness:** Give your hive a final thorough cleaning, removing any debris, wax drippings, or potential pest signs. Remember, bees thrive in a clean and healthy environment.

Location, location, location! Your bees deserve a haven that offers both comfort and security. Consider these key factors:

- **Shelter:** Protect your hive from direct sun, wind, and rain. Ideally, aim for partial shade with morning sun exposure for temperature regulation.
- **Accessibility:** Choose a spot that allows you to easily access the hive for inspections and management. Remember, beekeeping involves regular interaction.
- **Cleanliness:** Avoid placing the hive near garbage, pesticides, or other potential sources of contamination. Keep your buzzing friends safe and healthy!
- **Peace and Quiet:** Locate the hive away from high foot traffic, loud noises, or strong chemical smells. Your bees need a calm and peaceful environment to thrive.
- **Natural Resources:** Ideally, locate the hive near flowering plants and water sources. This provides easy access to nectar, pollen, and water, essential for their survival and honey production.

With everything meticulously prepared and the timing perfect, it's time to welcome your bees! Remember, gentleness is key. Follow your chosen introduction method carefully, avoiding unnecessary disturbances. Observe their initial behavior – are they exploring calmly, clustering around the queen? Patience and a watchful eye are essential during this crucial phase.

Additional Tips:

- **Mark your calendar:** Note the introduction date and monitor the hive activity over the next few days. This helps assess their adjustment and identify any potential issues early on.
- **Respect their space:** Avoid excessive peeking or manipulations during the first few days. Let them settle in and acclimate to their new surroundings.
- **Minimize stress:** Be mindful of loud noises, strong smells, or sudden movements near the hive. Create a calm and welcoming environment for your new residents.
- **Slow and Steady:** Move slowly and deliberately around the hive, avoiding sudden gestures or loud noises. Let your movements become familiar and predictable.
- **Minimal Smoke:** While some beekeepers use smoke to calm bees during inspections, it's not always necessary. Consider alternative methods like using a bee brush or simply moving slowly and confidently.

By following these guidelines and ensuring their new home is bee-ready, you'll foster a smooth transition and set the stage for a successful and rewarding beekeeping adventure!

Part 2

Beekeeping Throughout the Seasons

CHAPTER 4

SPRING AWAKENING

Winter's chill recedes, the sun warms the land, and a familiar hum fills the air – spring has arrived! This season signifies a resurgence of life in the beehive, a time for growth, expansion, and honey-making dreams taking flight.

In this chapter, we delve into the exciting world of spring beekeeping. You'll learn how to navigate this crucial period, from the first post-winter hive inspection to the strategic management of swarming behavior.

Firstly, we'll equip you with the skills to conduct a thorough spring hive inspection. Learn how to assess colony health, check for signs of disease or pests, and evaluate brood production and queen activity. You'll gain the confidence to interpret these vital signs and ensure your bees have a strong foundation for the busy season ahead.

Next, we'll explore techniques to encourage early brood production and colony growth. Discover essential practices like providing supplemental pollen and feeding strategies to boost bee energy and stimulate the queen's egg-laying. You'll learn how to create an environment that promotes rapid colony expansion and sets the stage for a bountiful honey harvest.

However, with growth comes the potential for swarming. Don't worry, beekeeper! This chapter equips you with the knowledge to anticipate and manage swarming behavior effectively. We'll delve into the reasons behind swarming, discuss various preventative measures, and explore methods for creating splits if necessary. You'll learn how to handle this natural phenomenon calmly and confidently, ensuring the continued health and productivity of your apiary.

Remember, spring is a season of immense change and activity within the hive. This chapter equips you with the skills and knowledge to navigate this exciting period, nurture your bees to thrive, and witness the wonders of a colony buzzing back to life! So, grab your hive tool, open your mind to the season's possibilities, and prepare to be amazed by the transformative power of spring in the beehive.

Inspecting hives after winter and assessing colony health

The days lengthen, the sun warms, and nature stirs awake – a sure sign that spring has sprung in your apiary too! As your bees buzz with renewed energy, it's time for your first hive inspection of the season – an exciting moment to reconnect with your colony and ensure their well-being after the long winter slumber. But don't worry, new beekeeper! This isn't about poking and prodding – it's a gentle observation to assess their health and set them up for a thriving spring and summer.

Before diving in, remember, timing is crucial. Honey bees follow their own brood cycle, so wait until stable temperatures (usually above 50°F/10°C for several days) encourage consistent brood rearing. Check with experienced beekeepers in your region for recommended inspection times, as weather patterns can vary. Remember, disturbing bees unnecessarily can stress them out, so choose a calm, sunny day when they're actively foraging.

Remember your trusty bee suit? Time to dust it off and become a spring guardian for your buzzing friends! Ensure your suit, veil, and gloves are in good condition, offering maximum protection and comfort. Pack essential tools like a hive tool for gentle prying, a frame lifter for easy handling, and a soft-bristled brush to gently nudge bees off frames. Use smoker responsibly and sparingly, minimizing smoke exposure for both you and your bees. Remember, gentle movements and calmness are key to a peaceful inspection.

With everything prepared, carefully remove the hive cover and inner cover, taking a moment to observe the overall activity level. Are bees bustling about? Is the entrance well-guarded? Now, slowly and systematically remove frames, observing bee behavior as you go. Are they calm and clustered, indicating a healthy queen? Are there signs of pests or disease? Look for healthy brood patterns, a mix of capped and uncapped, and assess the amount of honey stores. Remember, minimal disturbance is key, so work quickly and efficiently.

Now comes the detective work! Focus on key indicators of colony health:

- **Brood:** Look for healthy, compact patterns of capped and uncapped brood, indicating a productive queen. Irregularities might suggest issues.
- **Honey Stores:** Are frames well-filled, ensuring enough food for the growing colony? If not, supplemental feeding might be necessary.
- **The Queen:** Spotting her can be tricky, but keep an eye out for a larger bee with a longer abdomen. Queen markers can help identify her easily.

Don't just observe – document! jot down your findings about brood health, queen presence, honey stores, and any potential concerns. Create a hive inspection checklist or use a beekeeping journal to track changes over time. This information will be invaluable for future inspections and informed management decisions.

Noticing something off? Don't panic! Early intervention is key. Weak colonies, queenlessness, or pest infestations might require specific actions. Research solutions, consult experienced beekeepers, and never hesitate to seek help from beekeeping associations. Remember, beekeeping is a learning journey, and every challenge is an opportunity to grow.

Finally, give your bees a spring makeover! Gently remove debris and unwanted materials from the hive, address minor repairs, and ensure proper ventilation. Think of it as creating a sparkling spring home for your happy, healthy colony.

Inspecting your hives after winter is a crucial step towards a successful beekeeping season. By following these steps, being observant, and approaching your bees with respect and care, you'll gain valuable insights, ensure their well-being, and witness the wonders of their spring awakening firsthand.

Encouraging early brood production and colony growth

Spring unfolds, the sun warms, and your beehives buzz with renewed energy. This is the perfect time to set your bees up for a burst of growth, ensuring a strong colony throughout the season. Imagine your hives teeming with healthy broods, laying the foundation for abundant honey production and a thriving apiary. But how do you encourage this springtime boom? Worry not, new beekeeper! Here's your guide to nurturing early brood production and witnessing the magic of your colony's rapid expansion.

Think of your hive as a bee apartment building. To encourage tenants (baby bees!), ensure it's comfortable and well-stocked.

- **Food Stores:** Are there enough honey and pollen reserves? If not, consider supplemental feeding with sugar syrup and pollen patties.
- **Temperature:** Think "Goldilocks" – not too hot, not too cold. Proper ventilation is key for maintaining the ideal temperature range for brood rearing.
- **Health Check:** Rule out any diseases or pests that might hinder growth. Address issues promptly to create a healthy environment for your buzzing friends.

Imagine offering your bees a delicious energy drink! Stimulative feeding with sugar syrup provides a temporary boost during spring, encouraging the queen to lay more eggs.

- **Weigh the pros and cons:** Stimulative feeding can be helpful, but overdoing it can stress bees. Research and understand the potential drawbacks before diving in.
- **Sweet choices:** Choose appropriate sugar syrup recipes and feeding methods. Remember, natural resources like blooming flowers are always best when available.
- **Listen to your bees:** Monitor their response and adjust feeding strategies as needed. Don't force-feed – let their needs guide you.

Your queen bee is the heart of the hive, responsible for laying all those precious eggs. Here's how to support her:

- **Queen Check:** Assess her health and activity level. Is she laying well? If not, consider replacing her following best practices.

51

- **Introducing New Royalty (Optional):** If replacing the queen, ensure proper introduction methods to avoid colony rejection.
- **Queen Excluders (Optional):** These can be used strategically to manage brood production, but understand their purpose and potential drawbacks before using them.

Think of pollen as the protein powder for baby bees! Ensure they have enough for healthy development.

- **Pollen Powerhouse:** Natural pollen sources like blooming flowers are ideal. If scarce, consider pollen patties or supplements.
- **DIY Pollen Trap (Optional):** Get creative! You can set up a pollen trap to collect pollen from strong colonies and redistribute it to others in need.

Remember, beekeeping is about observation and adaptation.

- **Regular check-ups:** Inspect your hives regularly, monitoring brood patterns and overall colony activity.
- **Adapt and adjust:** Based on your observations, adapt your feeding strategies, queen management, or other methods to optimize colony growth.
- **Seek guidance:** Don't hesitate to seek help from experienced beekeepers or beekeeping associations if you have questions or concerns.

By following these tips and fostering a supportive environment, you'll witness the wonder of your bees' early brood production and colony growth. Remember, patience, observation, and respect are key ingredients for a successful spring awakening in your apiary.

Managing swarming behavior and preventing splits

Spring bursts forth, your bees buzz with renewed energy, and life hums within your hives. But amidst this joyful activity, a natural phenomenon sometimes arises – swarming. Imagine thousands of bees taking flight, swirling in a mesmerizing cloud, searching for a new home. While fascinating, swarming can present a challenge for new beekeepers. But fear not! Understanding why bees swarm and taking proactive steps can help you maintain a stable, thriving apiary.

Swarming is a bee colony's natural way to reproduce. When a hive becomes overcrowded, has an older queen, or lacks resources, the worker bees prepare for the "big move." Thousands gather around a new queen, ready to establish a new home. While it sounds dramatic, remember, swarming is not necessarily bad. It's a sign of a healthy, productive colony!

The good news? You can often prevent swarming by creating a happy, comfortable environment for your bees. Here are some tips:

- **Spacious digs:** Give your bees room to grow! Add supers or use larger hive bodies to avoid overcrowding.
- **Queen power:** A young, active queen is less likely to trigger swarming. Regularly assess your queen's health and consider replacing her if needed.
- **Feast time:** Ensure your bees have enough honey and pollen stores, especially during spring. Consider supplemental feeding if resources are scarce.
- **Ventilation matters:** Proper ventilation helps maintain cool temperatures within the hive, another factor influencing swarming behavior.

Even with your best efforts, sometimes a swarm happens. Don't panic! Here's how to handle it calmly and humanely:

- **Spot the signs:** Increased activity around the hive entrance and clusters of bees outside are telltale signs.
- **Bee-safe capture:** Use gentle methods like hiving boxes or swarm traps to capture the swarm, prioritizing the safety of both bees and yourself. Seek help from experienced beekeepers if needed.

Instead of letting nature take its course, you can consider planned splits, dividing a strong colony into two. This gives your bees more space and you, new colonies! However, splitting requires careful planning and specific conditions. Consult experienced beekeepers or beekeeping associations before deciding if this is the right approach for you. Remember, there's no one-size-fits-all answer to managing swarming. Weigh the pros and cons of prevention versus controlled splits, considering your long-term beekeeping goals and colony needs.

By understanding swarming behavior, taking preventative measures, and responding calmly to unforeseen situations, you can ensure a harmonious spring in your apiary, allowing your bees to thrive and you to witness the wonders of their bustling world.

CHAPTER 5

THE BUZZING SUMMER

Summer arrives, cloaking the land in sunshine and painting the meadows with vibrant blooms. For beekeepers, this season heralds a symphony of activity – a time of honey production, bustling colonies, and the sweet reward of your beekeeping endeavors.

This chapter equips you to navigate the whirlwind of summer beekeeping. You'll learn the art of monitoring honey production, ensuring your bees have ample space and resources to thrive. We'll delve into techniques for identifying and diagnosing potential bee diseases and pests, empowering you to keep your apiary healthy and thriving.

Firstly, we'll explore the delicate balance of managing hive space. Learn how to assess honey production, add supers when necessary, and optimize hive configuration for optimal bee health and honey storage. You'll discover the tools and techniques to ensure your bees have enough room to work their magic without feeling cramped or restricted.

But summer isn't without its challenges. This chapter dives into the world of identifying and diagnosing potential bee diseases and pests. While intimidating at first, we'll equip you with the knowledge and resources to recognize common threats and take informed action. Learn about symptoms, preventive measures, and treatment options, ensuring your colony stays healthy and productive throughout the season.

So, grab your bee suit, embrace the vibrant energy of summer, and prepare to witness the honey-making marvels unfold! This chapter equips you with the knowledge and confidence to manage the buzzing summer season, ensuring your bees thrive and you reap the delicious rewards of their hard work.

Monitoring honey production

The summer sun bathes your apiary in warmth, and your bees are abuzz with activity. This is the season of golden bounty, when nature's nectar transforms into the delicious treasure we know as honey. But how do you monitor this production and ensure your bees have the space they need to thrive? Worry not, new beekeeper! This guide will equip you with the knowledge to witness the wonder of honey making while keeping your colony happy and healthy.

Imagine your bees as tiny alchemists, converting flower nectar into liquid gold. Different flowers bloom at different times, creating honey flow periods unique to your region. Think of it as a bee buffet! The type and abundance of these flowers directly influence the amount and flavor of your honey. Observing your bees' foraging activity and identifying local blooms can give you valuable clues about your honey harvest.

Now, how do you know how much honey your bees are making? Here are some handy tips:

- **Hive Scales (Optional):** These amazing tools directly measure hive weight, providing precise honey production data.
- **Regular Inspections:** Take a peek inside your supers (honey storage boxes) and frames. Capped honey cells, like tiny golden domes, indicate it's ready for harvest.

- **Beekeeping Journal:** Become a beekeeping detective! Record your observations, honey flow periods, and harvest amounts. This data will be invaluable for future seasons.

As your bees fill their supers, space becomes crucial. Look for signs of overcrowding like a "bee beard" (bees clustered outside the hive entrance) or increased activity. Here's how to keep things spacious:

- **Adding Supers:** Think of them as apartment expansions! Add them strategically, considering honey flow and colony strength.
- **Queen Excluder (Optional):** This tool restricts the queen to the brood chamber, allowing honey production to focus in the supers. Remember, use it strategically and understand its purpose before placing it.

Imagine a honey-making relay race! By rotating supers, you encourage bees to fill new frames while harvesting ripe honey. Here's the key:

- **Identify Capped Frames:** Only fully capped honey is ready for harvest. Uncapped honey is still being processed by the bees.
- **Responsible Extraction:** Use sustainable practices and proper equipment to extract honey without harming your bees.

While abundant honey is exciting, remember, your bees' well-being is paramount. Excessive honey storage can lead to ventilation problems and overcrowding. So:

- **Monitor and Manage:** Don't wait until overcrowding becomes an issue. Harvest honey responsibly and create space for your bees to thrive.
- **Long-Term Sustainability:** Remember, beekeeping is about more than just honey. Prioritize the health and happiness of your colony for a successful and fulfilling beekeeping journey.

By understanding honey production, implementing clever monitoring strategies, and managing hive space effectively, you can enjoy the fruits of your bees' labor while ensuring their well-being throughout the buzzing summer months.

Identifying and diagnosing potential bee diseases and pests

Summer's warmth brings abundant blooms, buzzing activity, and, unfortunately, potential threats to your bee colony. While diseases and pests might sound scary, remember, early detection and informed action are key to keeping your bees healthy and thriving. Don't worry, new beekeeper! This guide will equip you with the knowledge to recognize potential issues, take proactive steps, and navigate any challenges that may arise.

Think of yourself as a bee detective! Observing your bees' behavior and the condition of your hive is crucial for early detection. Here's what to watch for:

- **Unusual Activity:** Are your bees lethargic, disoriented, or exhibiting abnormal behaviors like excessive aggression or shaking? These could be signs of trouble.
- **Visual Clues:** Keep an eye out for deformed bees, brood with unusual discoloration or spotting, or excessive debris around the hive entrance.
- **Seasonal Awareness:** Remember, some bee behaviors vary seasonally. Learn the natural rhythms of your colony to avoid mistaking normal activity for a problem.

While there are various bee diseases and pests, some are more common than others. Here's a brief overview of a few key threats:

- **American Foulbrood (AFB):** This bacterial disease attacks bee larvae, causing deformed brood and a foul odor. It's highly contagious and requires immediate action.
- **European Foulbrood (EFB):** Another bacterial disease affecting larvae, EFB causes sunken, discolored brood and a sour smell. Early intervention is crucial.

- **Varroa Mites:** These tiny parasites attach to adult bees, weakening them and transmitting diseases. Regular monitoring and treatment are vital for colony health.
- **Small Hive Beetle (SHB):** This destructive beetle attacks brood and honey stores, weakening colonies. Timely detection and management are essential.

This information is for awareness purposes only. If you suspect a disease or pest infestation, consult experienced beekeepers or beekeeping associations for proper diagnosis and treatment recommendations.

Sometimes, a closer look is needed. Here are some helpful tools:

- **Visual Inspections:** Regularly examine your bees, brood, and hive components for visual signs of abnormalities.
- **Brood Sample Analysis:** Submitting brood samples to professional labs can confirm specific diseases.
- **Mite Counts:** For Varroa monitoring, specialized methods like sugar roll tests can help assess mite levels.

Remember, you're not alone! The beekeeping community is here to support you:

- **Share and Learn:** Connect with other beekeepers to share experiences, ask questions, and learn from each other's successes and challenges.
- **Beekeeping Associations:** These invaluable resources offer educational programs, guidance, and support from experienced beekeepers.
- **Responsible Practices:** By following best practices and reporting suspected diseases, you contribute to the overall health of the bee population.

By staying vigilant, taking preventative measures, and seeking help when needed, you can ensure your bees enjoy a healthy, productive summer. Remember, with knowledge, dedication, and the support of the beekeeping community, you can navigate any challenges and witness the wonders of your thriving colony all season long.

CHAPTER 6

AUTUMN ABUNDANCE

As summer's warmth fades and leaves paint the landscape in hues of gold and russet, autumn arrives, marking a season of abundance in the beehive. Honeycombs brim with the golden reward of your bees' efforts, and it's time to celebrate the fruits of your beekeeping journey with the honey harvest. But with autumn comes the responsibility of preparing your colony for the harsh winter slumber ahead.

This chapter guides you through the essential steps of autumn beekeeping, from the exciting honey harvest to the crucial preparations for winter survival. You'll learn the art of extracting, straining, and processing your honey, ensuring a delicious and rewarding experience.

Firstly, we'll delve into the world of honey harvesting. Learn about different extraction methods, equipment choices, and proper handling techniques to preserve the quality and purity of your honey. This section equips you with the knowledge and confidence to confidently gather and process the sweet fruits of your bees' labor.

But harvest isn't the end of the story. Autumn is also the time to focus on colony health and winter preparations. We'll explore crucial steps like feeding your bees to replenish their energy reserves, monitoring for potential threats, and ensuring their queen lays enough eggs for a strong overwintering population. You'll learn how to assess your colony's needs and provide the support they require to survive the cold months ahead.

Finally, the chapter culminates with the art of winterizing your hives. Learn about essential tasks like ventilation adjustments, insulation strategies, and protecting against moisture and pests. By properly preparing your hives for winter, you ensure your bees have a safe and comfortable haven to weather the cold and emerge healthy and vibrant in the spring.

Remember, autumn is a season of transition and preparation. This chapter equips you with the knowledge and confidence to harvest your honey with pride, support your colony's health, and winterize your hives effectively. By following these steps, you ensure your bees thrive through the harsh winter and return stronger and more vibrant in the spring, ready to buzz into another exciting season of beekeeping!

Preparing for the honey harvest: extracting, straining, and processing

As autumn paints the landscape in fiery hues, your beehives hum with the culmination of their summer's work – a golden treasure: honey! This chapter will guide you through the exciting process of harvesting, processing, and savoring this liquid gold, ensuring your efforts reward you with delicious results and happy, healthy bees.

Imagine honey as a delicious fruit! Just like any fruit, it needs time to ripen before it's perfect for harvest. Unripe honey can be watery and prone to fermentation, so knowing the signs of ripeness is crucial. Look for capped frames – a telltale sign the bees have sealed them with a waxy lid. The "bounce test" is another handy trick: gently tilt a frame – ripe honey shouldn't drip or dribble. Remember, different honey flow periods can affect ripeness, so observe your bees and consult experienced beekeepers if needed.

Now, how do you get your hands on that delicious honey? There are different ways to approach this:

- **Manual Frame Removal:** This classic method involves carefully lifting frames from the hive and brushing off any bees. It's perfect for small-scale harvests and gives you a close look at your colony's health.
- **Hive Tool:** For more efficient frame removal, use a specialized hive tool to gently pry them loose. Be mindful of the bees and their delicate work.
- **Bee Vacuum (Optional):** This advanced method uses a vacuum to remove bees from frames before harvesting. It requires specific equipment and experience, so consider your needs and comfort level.

Once you have your frames, it's time to extract the honey! For smaller harvests, a manual extractor might be perfect. Imagine a giant merry-go-round for frames – spin it gently, and honey flows out! Remember, slow and steady wins the race here. If you have larger harvests, an electric extractor can save time and effort. But always prioritize safety: follow the manufacturer's instructions and wear protective gear.

Think of straining as giving your honey a spa treatment! It removes any wax particles, bee parts, or debris that might have made their way in. You can use a simple cheesecloth, a double sieve, or specialized honey filters. Choose the right mesh size based on how clear you want your honey. Remember, some people prefer a more rustic look with a few flecks of wax, while others like it crystal-clear.

Now, the big question: to heat or not to heat? Raw honey retains all its natural enzymes and flavors, but it might crystallize faster. Pasteurized honey stays smooth longer but loses some of its delicate taste and nutrients. The choice is yours! Once you've decided, choose high-quality food-grade containers for bottling and store your honey in a cool, dark place to preserve its quality.

Don't panic if your honey starts to solidify – it's not spoilage! Honey naturally crystallizes over time, especially raw honey. It's simply sugar returning to its solid state. Different types of honey crystallize differently – some become creamy, others form large crystals. If you prefer it liquid again, gently warm it up in a water bath – never directly over heat!

Honey isn't just for spreading on toast! Experiment with its versatility in the kitchen:

- **Baking:** Honey adds sweetness and moisture to cakes, cookies, and breads.
- **Sauces and glazes:** Drizzle honey over roasted vegetables, meats, or tofu for a delicious glaze.
- **Marinades:** Honey tenderizes meat and adds a subtle sweetness to savory dishes.
- **Cocktails and mocktails:** A touch of honey adds depth and complexity to drinks.

Remember, honey is also a natural antibacterial and medicinal remedy. Soothe a sore throat with a spoonful or use it for topical skin care treatments.

The journey from hive to home is filled with learning, observation, and the sweet reward of your bees' hard work. By following these tips and exploring your creativity, you can enjoy your honey harvest in countless ways, celebrating the magic of beekeeping and the bounty of nature.

Feeding bees for winter and supporting colony health

As autumn leaves pirouette to the ground, your beekeeping journey takes a turn towards caring for your bees through the colder months. Just like we prepare for winter, our buzzing friends need our support to ensure they have the resources and environment to thrive until spring's warmth returns. This guide will equip you with the knowledge and practical tips to nourish your bees, optimize their health, and create a cozy haven for a peaceful winter rest.

Imagine your bees as tiny gourmands stocking up for a long winter. Ideally, they've been busy all summer collecting nectar and pollen, filling their combs with golden honey – their main winter food source. But how do you know if they have enough?

- **Capped Frames:** Look for frames completely sealed with wax – a telltale sign they're full of honey.
- **Weighty Hives:** Regularly weigh your hives. A steady or increasing weight indicates abundant stores.
- **Active Brood Production:** A healthy brood pattern demonstrates the colony's strength and ability to sustain itself.

If you observe empty frames, decreased activity, or a weak brood pattern, don't wait! Early assessment and intervention are crucial for a successful winter.

Think of winter feeding as giving your bees a helping hand. Here are some common options:

- **Sugar Syrup:** Easy to make and readily available, but lacks pollen's essential nutrients. Use a 1:1 ratio of sugar and water.
- **Fondant:** A slow-release, high-energy paste, ideal for colder climates. Choose commercially prepared fondant specifically for bees.
- **Pollen Patties:** Packed with protein and vitamins, they mimic natural pollen sources. Ensure they're fresh and free of contaminants.
- **Dry Pollen Substitute:** A pollen alternative, especially valuable in regions with limited pollen availability. Opt for reputable brands and follow mixing instructions carefully.

While convenient, feeding honey for winter is generally not recommended due to potential disease risks and nutritional imbalances. Consult experienced beekeepers for guidance if considering this option.

Now, how do you get the food to your bees? Different feeder types have their pros and cons:

- **Internal Feeders:** Placed inside the hive, they offer direct access but might be more challenging to manage.
- **External Feeders:** Easier to access and refill, but ensure they're protected from weather and pests.

- **Inverted Jars (Optional):** A budget-friendly option, but requires careful setup to avoid leaks and drowning bees.

No matter the feeder type, prioritize:

- **Placement:** Choose locations readily accessible to bees within the hive or protected from harsh weather outside.
- **Hygiene:** Thoroughly clean and disinfect feeders before use and regularly throughout the season.
- **Quality:** Use high-quality ingredients and follow recommended mixing ratios to ensure proper nutrition.

Food is crucial, but it's not the only factor for happy, healthy winter bees:

- **Ventilation:** Proper ventilation prevents moisture buildup and promotes healthy air circulation within the hive.
- **Minimal Disruptions:** Limit hive inspections during winter to conserve bee energy. Only check for emergencies or urgent needs.
- **Varroa Mite Control:** Implement effective varroa mite control measures throughout the season, especially before winter, to minimize parasite pressure.
- **Optional Insulation:** In colder climates, consider adding insulation (e.g., natural materials like pine needles) around the hive to help bees regulate temperature.

Remember, specific strategies might vary depending on your region's climate and preferred hive type (Langstroth, Top Bar, etc.). Do your research and adapt techniques based on your unique context. By following these tips and providing your bees with the care they need, you can create a haven for them to weather the winter months peacefully, ensuring a vibrant and healthy colony ready to welcome spring's bloom.

Winterizing hives for successful overwintering

As autumn paints the world in fiery hues, it's time to turn our attention to our buzzing friends - the bees! While we snuggle up with cozy blankets, our bees face the challenge of surviving the colder months. But fear not, new beekeeper! By winterizing your hives, you can create a safe and comfortable haven for your colony, ensuring they emerge in spring happy, healthy, and ready to buzz forth.

Think of your hive as a cozy cabin for your bees. Before winter sets in, it's crucial to identify any potential weaknesses:

- **Inspect for Cracks and Gaps:** Check every nook and cranny for damage, loose fittings, or gaps that could let in drafts or unwanted guests. Remember, even tiny openings can be problematic!
- **Drafty Doors?** The hive entrance is crucial for airflow, but drafts can be harmful. Check if the entrance needs adjusting or if a smaller entrance reducer (a special insert) is needed for your climate.
- **Moisture Matters:** Too much moisture can lead to mold and disease. Look for signs of water damage or condensation, and make sure your hive has proper ventilation.

Imagine the hive entrance as a door for your bees. It lets fresh air in and keeps predators out, but it shouldn't be drafty!

- **Entrance Reducers:** These handy tools help regulate airflow and deter pests like mice. Choose the right size for your climate and colony strength. Remember, proper ventilation is vital even with a smaller entrance.
- **Striking the Balance:** While protecting your bees is important, remember they still need fresh air. Ensure your hive isn't sealed too tightly, even with insulation (more on that later!).

Think of insulation as an extra layer of warmth for your beehive. Depending on your climate, you might consider:

- **Natural Materials:** Packing around the hive with straw, leaves, or wood shavings can provide some insulation. Opt for breathable materials and ensure proper ventilation is maintained.
- **Commercial Wraps:** These wraps reflect heat back into the hive, offering additional protection in colder climates. Choose breathable materials and follow installation instructions carefully.
- **Double-Walled Hives:** These specialized hives offer built-in insulation, simplifying winter preparation. Consider their cost and suitability for your needs.

Moisture is the enemy of a happy winter hive! Here's how to keep things dry and cozy:

- **Ventilation is Key:** Proper airflow helps prevent moisture buildup. Ensure your hive has adequate ventilation even with insulation. Consider screened bottom boards for additional moisture control.
- **Absorbent Materials:** Placing dry, absorbent materials like wood chips or pine needles inside the hive can help trap moisture. Replace them regularly to prevent mold growth.
- **Hive Placement:** Positioning your hive in a sunny, well-drained location can help minimize moisture issues.

While your bees sleep, some unwelcome visitors might try to crash their winter party! Here's how to keep them out:

- **Know Your Enemies:** Different regions have different hive predators. Research common threats in your area, like mice, skunks, or birds.
- **Hardware Cloth:** This strong mesh can be used to block hive entrances from larger predators. Ensure it's securely attached and doesn't restrict airflow.
- **Mouse Guards:** These clever contraptions allow bees to enter but deter mice. Install them correctly for maximum effectiveness.
- **Hive Placement:** Choose a location away from potential predator hiding spots and consider using elevated hive stands for added security.

Vigilance is key! Regularly monitor your hives throughout winter and adapt your defenses if needed. Remember, specific winterizing approaches might vary depending on your climate and preferred hive type. Research and adapt techniques based on your unique context. By following these tips and tailoring them to your specific needs, you can create a winter haven for your bees. As spring arrives, you'll be rewarded with a thriving colony buzzing with life, ready to embark on a new season of wonder, their wings vibrant with the promise of renewed nectar, pollen, and the vital role they play in the dance of life.

Part 3

Advanced Beekeeping Practices

CHAPTER 7

EXPANDING YOUR APIARY

Congratulations, beekeeper! You've mastered the basics, nurtured a thriving colony, and tasted the sweet rewards of your beekeeping journey. But the adventure doesn't stop there! This chapter unveils the exciting world of expanding your apiary, transforming your single hive into a bustling bee empire.

Whether you dream of multiplying your honey harvest, diversifying your beekeeping experience, or simply witnessing the wonders of multiple colonies thriving side-by-side, this chapter equips you with the knowledge and skills to confidently expand your apiary.

Firstly, we'll delve into the world of colony multiplication. Learn about various techniques for creating splits, effectively dividing your existing colony into two healthy units. Discover different splitting methods, understand the optimal timing, and master the essential steps to ensure the success of your new colonies.

But creating new colonies is just the beginning. We'll also explore the fascinating world of raising your own queens. Learn about queen rearing techniques, from selecting breeder stock to grafting larvae and managing queen cells. Whether you prefer purchasing queens or want the satisfaction of rearing your own, this chapter empowers you to make informed decisions and contribute to the long-term genetic diversity of your apiary.

Managing multiple hives brings its own set of considerations. We'll discuss the important factors to remember when planning and managing multiple hives. Learn about optimal apiary layout, considerations for different locations, and essential strategies for keeping track of colony health and honey production across your expanding bee empire.

Remember, with greater beekeeping comes greater responsibility. This chapter concludes by highlighting the legal and regulatory requirements applicable to beekeepers. Understand your local regulations regarding apiary registration, disease control, and responsible beekeeping practices. Ensuring compliance not only protects your bees but also fosters a positive image for the beekeeping community as a whole.

So, dust off your bee suit, embrace the excitement of expansion, and prepare to witness the wonders of multiple colonies buzzing with life! This chapter equips you with the knowledge and confidence to navigate the journey of expanding your apiary, ensuring your bee empire thrives and you continue to experience the joy and rewards of responsible beekeeping.

Techniques for creating splits and raising new queens

As your confidence and beekeeping knowledge blossom, you might start contemplating expanding your apiary – creating new hives and nurturing vibrant colonies. This chapter delves into two advanced techniques: creating splits and raising new queens. Remember, these are advanced practices requiring careful planning and experience. But fear not! We'll explore the core concepts and considerations to guide you on your exciting beekeeping journey.

Imagine your beehive as a bustling city. When it gets crowded, sometimes a new "neighborhood" (a split) might be the answer. This natural phenomenon, called swarming, is how colonies reproduce. While fascinating, planned splits offer more control and can be beneficial for:

- **Colony health:** Reducing overcrowding prevents stress and potential diseases.
- **Increased honey production:** More colonies mean more honey (potentially)!
- **Introducing new genetics:** Introducing new queens promotes genetic diversity and colony strength.

Remember, planned splits require careful planning and experience. Consult experienced beekeepers and thoroughly research before diving in.

Think of splitting as giving your bees a fresh start. But choosing the right moment is crucial! Here's what to consider:

- **Population:** Your colony should be strong and populous, with plenty of bees to support two hives.
- **Brood Pattern:** Look for a healthy brood pattern with all stages present, indicating a thriving queen.
- **Honey Stores:** Both the new and original hive need ample honey reserves to survive until the next nectar flow.
- **Seasonality:** Spring or early summer is often ideal, allowing enough time for new colonies to establish themselves before winter.

There are different ways to split a colony, each with its advantages. Remember, these are advanced techniques, so proceed with caution and guidance:

- **Walker Split:** This popular method involves dividing the brood, frames, and bees between two hives, creating balanced new colonies.
- **Demaree Split:** This technique uses queen excluders to manipulate brood rearing and create a new queen before splitting.
- **Other Splitting Methods:** More complex methods like mini splits or nucleus splits exist, but require experience and specific equipment.

The queen bee is the heart of the colony. Sometimes, introducing a new queen is necessary for various reasons:

- **Age and Performance:** Queens naturally decline in egg-laying ability with age.
- **Disease Concerns:** Replacing a queen can help manage certain diseases.

Introducing a new queen requires specific techniques:

- **Caged Introduction:** The new queen is gradually introduced to the colony in a cage, allowing them to get used to her scent.
- **Push-in Introduction:** A faster method for experienced beekeepers, but requires careful handling.
- **Direct Release (Grafting):** Highly advanced technique involving raising your own queen, not recommended for beginners.

Raising your own queens is a fascinating but intricate skill. It requires specialized equipment, knowledge, and experience. Consider attending workshops or consulting experienced beekeepers before venturing into this advanced practice.

Queen excluders are grids that prevent the queen from moving between hive boxes. They have specific uses:

- Preventing the queen from laying eggs in supers: Useful for honey production.
- Confining the queen during splits: Can simplify some splitting methods.

However, queen excluders can also restrict queen movement and reduce brood production. Decide on their use based on your specific goals and management strategies.

Expanding your apiary through splits and queen management requires experience and careful planning. Consult experienced beekeepers, research thoroughly, and start small when venturing into these advanced techniques. As you gain confidence and knowledge, the rewards of nurturing thriving colonies will make your beekeeping journey even more fulfilling.

While this provides a general overview, specific approaches might vary depending on your region's climate and preferred hive type. Research and adapt techniques based on your unique context.

Considerations for managing multiple hives and apiary locations

Congratulations! Your passion for beekeeping has led you to consider nurturing multiple hives, expanding your apiary and becoming a true beekeeping maestro. While exciting, managing multiple hives and potentially even out-apiaries presents new challenges and considerations. This chapter will guide you through the key aspects of navigating this exciting growth phase, helping you ensure the well-being of your bees and the success of your apiary ventures.

Imagine yourself conducting an orchestra – with each hive being a unique instrument! Managing multiple hives requires strategic time management and organization. Here are some handy tips:

- **Plan and prioritize:** Create a weekly or monthly schedule for inspections, maintenance, and honey extraction.
- **Streamline your routine:** Invest in efficient tools like hive tools, smoker stands, and multi-frame extractors.
- **Delegate or seek help:** Don't be afraid to enlist the help of fellow beekeepers or family members for specific tasks.

Sometimes, expanding your apiary means setting up hives beyond your backyard. Choosing the right out-apiary location is crucial:

- **Forage feast:** Ensure access to diverse, year-round pollen and nectar sources within a 2-mile radius.
- **Accessibility matters:** Choose a location easily accessible for regular inspections and maintenance.
- **Know the rules:** Research and comply with local regulations regarding apiary placement and beekeeping practices.

Moving hives requires careful planning and attention to bee well-being:

- **Secure those frames:** Use straps, mesh, or specialized travel covers to prevent frames from shifting and harming bees.
- **Ventilation is key:** Ensure proper ventilation during transport to avoid overheating and stress.
- **Mind the weather:** Avoid transporting hives during extreme temperatures or windy conditions.

With more hives comes a greater responsibility to prevent disease spread:

- **Become a vigilant inspector:** Regularly monitor all hives for signs of disease and parasites.
- **Biosecurity is your shield:** Implement biosecurity measures like separate tools and equipment for each apiary.
- **Stay informed and stay connected:** Follow local beekeeping associations and report any suspected disease outbreaks promptly.

Detailed records are your secret weapon for managing multiple hives effectively:

- **Track key information:** Record inspection dates, honey production, queen information, and any treatments applied.
- **Consider digital tools:** Explore beekeeping apps or software for easy data organization and analysis.
- **Stay consistent:** Make record-keeping a regular habit to maintain a clear picture of your apiary's health and progress.

Expanding your apiary is a rewarding journey, but it requires careful planning, dedication, and continuous learning. Embrace the challenges, seek support from your beekeeping community, and most importantly, prioritize the well-being of your buzzing friends. With passion and knowledge, you'll be conducting a beautiful multi-hive symphony in no time, contributing to the health and harmony of your local beekeeping landscape.

Remember that specific regulations and requirements might vary depending on your region. It's crucial to research and comply with all local laws and regulations related to apiary management and beekeeping practices before expanding your apiary or setting up out-apiaries. Consult your local beekeeping association or relevant authorities for comprehensive guidance.

Responsibilities and regulations for beekeepers

As your passion for beekeeping flourishes, venturing into multiple hives or out-apiaries is an exciting step. But with great beekeeping power comes great responsibility! This chapter delves into the ethical, legal, and community-oriented aspects of expanding your apiary, ensuring your beekeeping journey is not only successful but also responsible and respectful.

Think of yourself as a bee guardian, nurturing not just your hives but contributing to the bigger picture. Beekeepers play a crucial role in:

- **Promoting bee health:** Responsible practices help prevent disease spread and support healthy bee populations.
- **Boosting biodiversity:** By providing pollen and nectar sources, your bees contribute to a thriving ecosystem.
- **Sustainable beekeeping:** Choosing responsible practices like local honey sources and eco-friendly hive materials benefits the environment and future generations of bees.

Remember, being a beekeeper extends beyond honey production. Embrace your role as an ambassador for these amazing creatures!

Every beekeeper superhero needs a rulebook! Before expanding your apiary, familiarize yourself with local and national beekeeping regulations. These might cover:

- **Hive registration and permitting:** Most areas require registering your hives and obtaining permits for apiary expansion.
- **Apiary placement restrictions:** Regulations might specify minimum distances from property lines, roads, or other apiaries.
- **Disease prevention and reporting:** Staying informed about reportable diseases and following reporting protocols is crucial.

Feeling overwhelmed? Don't fret! Start by contacting your local beekeeping association or relevant agricultural authorities. They can guide you through the legalities and ensure your apiary expansion is compliant.

Think of disease reporting as your beekeeping superpower! By promptly reporting suspected bee diseases, you help protect:

- **Your own bees:** Early detection and intervention can prevent devastating outbreaks in your apiary.
- **Other beekeepers:** Sharing information helps contain diseases and protect apiaries across your community.

Stay vigilant! Regularly inspect your hives and learn to recognize signs of common bee diseases. If you suspect something, don't hesitate to contact your local bee inspector or extension office. Remember, early action can make a world of difference!

Sharing your honey bounty is wonderful, but regulations ensure consumer safety and maintain beekeeping's integrity. Here's what you need to know:

- **Food safety regulations:** Most regions have specific regulations for honey labeling, processing, and storage.
- **Good hygiene practices:** Maintaining clean equipment and following proper honey extraction methods is crucial.
- **Traceability:** Keeping records of your honey's origin and processing steps is essential.

Feeling unsure? Don't worry! Resources are available to help you understand and comply with honey sales regulations. Talk to your local beekeeping association or food safety authorities for guidance. Remember, responsible honey production benefits everyone!

Happy bees, happy neighbors! As your apiary grows, consider the impact on your community:

- **Communicate openly:** Talk to your neighbors about your apiary, address any concerns, and educate them about the benefits of bees.
- **Responsible placement:** Choose locations mindful of potential disturbances to neighbors, like noise or bee traffic.
- **Bee-autiful solutions:** Consider planting bee-friendly flowers around your apiary to create a visually appealing and beneficial haven for your bees.

By fostering positive relationships, you can ensure your beekeeping journey thrives while being a good neighbor! The beekeeping world is constantly buzzing with new research and best practices. Stay informed and engaged by:

- **Joining beekeeping associations:** Connect with other beekeepers, learn from their experiences, and participate in educational workshops.
- **Staying updated on research:** Subscribe to beekeeping publications, follow relevant online forums, and attend industry events.
- **Advocating for bee health:** Support organizations working to protect bees and promote responsible beekeeping practices.

Remember, beekeeping is a lifelong learning journey. By staying informed and engaged, you can contribute to a thriving future for both bees and beekeepers!

Expanding your apiary isn't just about more hives; it's about embracing responsibility, knowledge, and community. With dedication and these guiding principles, you can be a responsible beekeeper, a good neighbor, and an advocate for the future of these fascinating creatures.

CHAPTER 8

HONEYBEE PRODUCTS BEYOND HONEY

Honey's sweetness may be the familiar face of beekeeping, but the resourceful honeybee offers a hidden trove beyond the familiar jar. This chapter opens the door to a world of niche beekeeping products and exciting value-added opportunities.

Prepare to explore the fascinating potential of beeswax, propolis, royal jelly, and pollen. We'll delve into harvesting, responsible practices, and their diverse applications, from traditional uses to modern health and wellness products.

But the journey doesn't stop there! Discover the potential of niche products like bee venom therapy kits, mead production, and even beekeeping experiences. This chapter equips you with the knowledge and inspiration to unlock the full potential of your beekeeping journey and explore the buzzing bounty beyond the honey barrel.

So, get ready to expand your horizons, diversify your offerings, and contribute to a sustainable future for bees and beekeepers alike! Buckle up and let's delve into the hive's hidden treasures!

Harvesting and using beeswax, propolis, royal jelly, and pollen

Honey isn't the only treasure our buzzing friends produce! Bees offer a diverse array of natural products, each with unique properties and potential benefits. This chapter whisks you on a journey beyond the golden jar, exploring the fascinating world of beeswax, propolis, royal jelly, and pollen. By understanding how to harvest these gifts responsibly and ethically, you can unlock a whole new level of beekeeping enjoyment and appreciation.

Beeswax: Nature's Versatile Wonder

Imagine tiny architects crafting intricate structures with a golden, fragrant material. That's beeswax, a natural wonder with numerous uses:

- **Composition:** This complex wax is primarily made by worker bees and boasts antibacterial and waterproofing properties.

- **Harvesting:** You can collect beeswax from cappings after honey extraction, use solar wax melters for a sustainable approach, or invest in specialized extractors for larger operations.
- **Unleashing its Magic:** From crafting beautiful candles and natural polishes to creating skincare products and food wraps, beeswax offers endless possibilities. Explore online resources and beekeeping communities for creative inspiration!

Propolis: Nature's Antibacterial Shield

Think of propolis as a beehive's natural defense system. This resinous substance, collected from plants by bees, has potential antibacterial and antioxidant properties:

- **Composition:** Propolis is a complex mixture with diverse components, and its properties might vary depending on the plant source.
- **Sustainable Harvesting:** Consider using hive inserts that allow bees to create propolis without disrupting their natural production. Always prioritize colony health over excessive harvesting.
- **Responsible Use:** Remember, propolis is not a magic cure-all and regulations often govern its use. Consult healthcare professionals before consuming propolis products and research reputable sources.

Royal Jelly: A Treasured Hive Product

Royal jelly, the food for queen bees, holds a certain mystique. While research explores its potential benefits, responsible harvesting is crucial:

- **Unique Role:** Royal jelly nourishes queen larvae and contributes to their longevity. Large-scale harvesting can harm queen health and colony development.
- **Ethical Considerations:** Consider alternative ways to support queen health, like providing diverse pollen sources and maintaining strong colonies.

- **Exploring Alternatives:** If choosing to harvest, prioritize minimal impact methods and prioritize colony well-being above personal gain.

Pollen: A Protein Powerhouse

Imagine tiny dust motes packed with protein, vitamins, and minerals. That's bee pollen, a nutritional powerhouse collected from flowers:

- **Nourishing Gift:** Pollen contributes to bee nutrition and can offer potential health benefits for humans when consumed responsibly.
- **Gathering Techniques:** Pollen traps placed at hive entrances collect pollen grains without harming bees. Explore different methods based on your needs and apiary setup.
- **Responsible Harvesting:** Remember, excessive pollen collection can impact colony health. Start small, monitor your hives, and prioritize their well-being over maximizing pollen yield.

As you delve into the world beyond honey, remember the incredible partnership you share with your bees. By harvesting their gifts responsibly and appreciating their vital role in our ecosystem, you become not just a beekeeper, but an advocate for their well-being and a steward of their natural bounty.

Exploring niche beekeeping products and value-added opportunities

Have you ever dreamt of expanding your beekeeping passion beyond the golden jar of honey? Well, buckle up, bee enthusiast, because the world of niche bee products and value-added opportunities is waiting to be explored! This chapter delves into the exciting realm beyond the mainstream, offering a glimpse into unique products, creative ventures, and the potential to turn your beekeeping hobby into something truly buzzworthy. Remember, venturing into this path requires research, planning, and responsible practices, but the rewards can be both personally fulfilling and contribute to a thriving beekeeping community.

Think beyond the typical suspects! The beehive offers a treasure trove of lesser-known products:

- **Drone brood:** Rich in protein and sometimes used in nutritional supplements (research regulations and ethical considerations!).
- **Bee venom:** With potential therapeutic uses, but beekeeping experience and proper training are crucial.
- **Apilarnil:** A royal jelly derivative with potential health benefits, but ethical harvesting is paramount.

Exploring these niche products is exciting, but remember: thorough research, understanding suitability and regulations, and prioritizing responsible and ethical practices are essential before diving in.

Let's unleash your inner alchemist! With creativity and knowledge, you can transform raw bee products into unique value-added offerings:

- **Infused honeys:** Experiment with herbs, spices, or fruits to create flavor sensations for every palate.
- **Handcrafted candles:** Capture the natural beauty and fragrance of beeswax in charming candles.
- **Natural soaps and cosmetics:** Harness the nourishing properties of honey, propolis, and beeswax to create luxurious pampering products.

Remember, understanding market trends, consumer preferences, and pricing strategies is key to making your value-added creations a success. Don't forget to explore pollination contracts or queen rearing for sale as potential service-based options!

It's time to discover your bee-tastic calling! Identify your:

- **Interests:** What excites you about beekeeping and its products?
- **Skills:** Are you a crafty candle maker, a marketing whiz, or a meticulous queen breeder?
- **Target audience:** Who are you hoping to reach with your offerings?

Market research, branding, and pricing strategies are your secret weapons here. Don't forget to explore resources and support networks for aspiring bee-based entrepreneurs!

Remember, your buzzing friends come first! Prioritize bee health and responsible harvesting practices in everything you do. Be mindful of overexploitation and its potential negative impacts. Source materials ethically, promote sustainable beekeeping, and educate others about responsible practices.

Before taking flight, make sure you have your paperwork in order:

- Comply with food safety regulations, labeling requirements, and relevant permits.
- Research local and national regulations specific to your niche products.
- Consult legal professionals or relevant authorities for guidance.

Remember, thorough preparation protects you, your customers, and the bees! Exploring niche beekeeping and value-added opportunities can be a rewarding journey of creativity, entrepreneurship, and connection to the fascinating world of bees. Remember, responsible practices, continuous learning, and a commitment to the well-being of your bees are the cornerstones of success. So, go forth, explore, and create something truly bee-autiful!

CHAPTER 9

TROUBLESHOOTING AND PROBLEM-SOLVING

Even the most experienced beekeeper encounters challenges and setbacks. While bees are amazing creatures, unexpected issues can arise, testing your knowledge and composure. But fear not! This chapter equips you with the essential skills and resources to become a confident beekeeping detective, diagnosing problems effectively and implementing solutions with expertise.

Forget frantic Googling and panicked phone calls. We'll equip you to identify common beekeeping issues and diseases, from varroa mites to queenlessness, understanding their symptoms and potential causes. Learn to read the signs your bees are sending, interpreting hive activity, brood patterns, and behavior to identify potential problems early on.

But diagnosis is just the first step. This chapter dives into implementing effective treatment and management strategies. Learn about various treatment options, their effectiveness, and responsible application practices. We'll discuss preventative measures, integrated pest management approaches, and natural solutions to maintain colony health and minimize the need for interventions.

Remember, you're not alone on this journey. We'll guide you to valuable resources and support systems available to beekeepers facing challenges. Discover online forums, beekeeping associations, professional bee inspectors, and other resources to connect with experienced beekeepers and access expert advice when needed.

So, take a deep breath, beekeeper! This chapter empowers you to confront challenges with confidence, transforming setbacks into learning opportunities and ensuring your bees thrive even when faced with unexpected hurdles. Remember, every challenge is an opportunity to deepen your understanding and become a more resourceful beekeeper. Let's turn those baffles into buzzes of success!

Diagnosing common beekeeping issues and diseases

Keeping your beehive buzzing with happy, healthy bees is every beekeeper's dream. But even the most dedicated beekeeper encounters challenges along the way. This chapter equips you with the knowledge and tools to confidently diagnose common beekeeping issues and diseases, ensuring your apiary thrives. Remember, early detection and intervention are key, so let's delve into the world of beekeeping detective work!

Think of yourself as a beehive detective! Regular, thorough inspections are your first line of defense. Here's why:

- **Observing is key:** Look closely at brood patterns, adult bee behavior, and hive components. Use a hive tool and smoker safely to get a good look.
- **Record your findings:** Keep a detailed log of your observations, noting any abnormalities or changes. This helps track progress and identify trends.
- **Be prepared:** Equip yourself with resources like beekeeping books, online guides, and photos of healthy hives for comparison.

Our buzzing friends are excellent communicators! Changes in their behavior can signal potential problems:

- **Lethargy or abnormal activity:** Are your bees less active than usual? Are they displaying aggression or unusual clustering? These could be signs of trouble.
- **Learn their language:** Observe healthy bee behavior and learn to recognize subtle changes that might indicate stress, disease, or other issues.
- **Resources are your friends:** Seek guidance from experienced beekeepers, beekeeping associations, or online resources to understand typical bee behavior patterns.

Just like in a detective story, there might be multiple suspects! Don't jump to conclusions:

- **Consider all possibilities:** Different issues can share similar symptoms. Research and compare potential causes before forming a diagnosis.
- **Seek expert advice:** Consult experienced beekeepers or consult diagnostic guides for in-depth information and accurate identification.

Once you've identified the culprit, it's time for action:

- **Treatment options:** Depending on the issue, various treatment methods might be available. Always prioritize responsible and approved treatment methods.
- **Prevention is key:** Strong colony management, proper hygiene, and maintaining healthy bee populations are your best defenses against future issues.

Remember, every beekeeper learns along the way:

- **Keep a log**: Document your troubleshooting experiences, including observations, challenges, and solutions. This helps you learn and improve.
- **Share your knowledge:** Join online forums, attend workshops, and connect with beekeeping associations. Sharing experiences and learning from others is invaluable.

By becoming a skilled beehive detective, you'll ensure your apiary thrives. Remember, with dedication, observation, and the support of the beekeeping community, you can overcome challenges and keep your bees buzzing happily ever after!

Implementing effective treatment and management strategies

Congratulations, beekeeper! You've identified the culprit behind your beehive woes. But the journey doesn't end with diagnosis. Now comes the crucial part: implementing effective treatment and management strategies to restore your apiary to its buzzing best. This chapter equips you with the knowledge and tools to approach bee health challenges responsibly, effectively, and with the well-being of your bees always in mind. Remember, successful treatment goes beyond just throwing treatments at the problem – it's about understanding the issue, tailoring solutions, and fostering a healthy hive environment. Let's dive in!

Think of yourself as a bee healthcare provider, prioritizing the well-being of your patients – the bees! Here's why responsible practices matter:

- **Choose wisely:** Opt for treatments that minimize harm to bees and the environment. Explore integrated pest management (IPM) strategies that combine preventive measures and natural solutions.
- **Knowledge is power:** Research treatment options, understand their mechanisms and potential side effects, and only use them when necessary and follow precise instructions.

No two beekeeping challenges are exactly alike. Here's a glimpse into tackling some common foes:

- **Swarming:** Consider queen management techniques, artificial swarm control methods, or creating splits when appropriate.
- **Queenlessness:** Explore options like introducing a new queen, encouraging supersedure, or uniting queenless hives.
- **Weak hives:** Investigate potential causes like pests, disease, inadequate resources, or poor queen performance. Implement targeted solutions like providing supplemental food, treating for pests, or introducing a new queen.
- **Pests and diseases:** Choose approved treatment methods based on the specific pest or disease, following recommended dosages and timelines meticulously. Remember, prevention is key – maintain strong colonies and proper hygiene to minimize future issues.

A healthy queen is the heart of a thriving hive. Consider these strategies:

- **Queen rearing:** Learn the basics of raising your own queens for long-term colony control and genetic selection.
- **Queen introductions:** Master the art of introducing new queens successfully to avoid colony rejection.
- **Supersedure:** Understand how natural queen replacement works and when to intervene for optimal colony health.

Remember, each technique requires specific knowledge and practice. Utilize resources like beekeeping associations, online tutorials, and experienced mentors to hone your queen management skills.

Think of balanced nutrition as the foundation for strong immune systems and disease resistance in your bees:

- Pollen patties, sugar syrup, and protein supplements: These can be helpful during dearth periods or for weak hives, but use them judiciously and only when needed.
- Balanced natural sources: Provide diverse pollen and nectar sources throughout the season for optimal nutrition.

Remember, excessive feeding can disrupt natural foraging behaviors and harm bee health. Consult experienced beekeepers for guidance on appropriate feeding practices.

Resources and support for beekeepers facing challenges

Even the most experienced beekeeper encounters challenges and setbacks. The good news is, you're not alone! This section equips you with a network of resources and support systems to help you navigate challenging situations with confidence and keep your bees thriving. Remember, beekeeping is a journey of continuous learning and growth, and sometimes, reaching out for help is the key to overcoming obstacles and achieving success.

Imagine a network of fellow beekeepers cheering you on, sharing their wisdom, and offering a helping hand. That's what local beekeeping associations offer! Here's why you should join:

- **Find your tribe:** Connect with beekeepers at all experience levels who share your passion and understand the challenges you face.
- **Learn from the best:** Attend workshops, demonstrations, and field days led by experienced beekeepers and industry experts.

- **Get mentored:** Find experienced beekeepers willing to guide you, answer your questions, and offer practical advice.

Finding your local association is easy! Search online directories, ask at beekeeping supply stores, or check local agricultural extension offices for upcoming meetings and events.

The internet is buzzing with valuable resources for beekeepers! Here are some popular options:

- **Beekeeping forums:** Connect with beekeepers worldwide, share challenges and solutions, and learn from diverse perspectives.
- **Educational websites and blogs:** Find articles, tutorials, and in-depth guides on every aspect of beekeeping.
- **Online communities and social media groups:** Join groups dedicated to specific beekeeping interests or regions for targeted support and discussions.

Remember, not all information online is created equal. Verify the credibility of sources, prioritize well-established beekeeping websites and organizations, and don't hesitate to ask experienced beekeepers for recommendations. Many government agencies and extension services offer valuable resources for beekeepers:

- **Disease prevention and control:** Access information on bee diseases, pest management strategies, and regulations.
- **Financial assistance programs:** In some cases, government programs might offer financial support for beekeeping activities or bee health initiatives.
- **Technical assistance:** Extension services often provide beekeeping workshops, technical advice, and diagnostic services.

Research your local and national government agencies for available resources and programs relevant to your needs.

Sometimes, complex challenges require expert intervention:

- **Professional bee inspectors:** Licensed professionals trained to diagnose bee diseases, recommend treatment plans, and ensure apiary compliance with regulations.
- **Bee health consultants:** Offer specialized expertise in diagnosing unusual problems, providing tailored treatment solutions, and optimizing bee health.

Consulting a professional can be invaluable, especially for complex issues, recurring problems, or apiaries with large populations. Don't hesitate to seek expert guidance when needed.

Stay ahead of the curve by tapping into the latest research advancements:

- **Leading beekeeping research institutions:** Explore their websites, publications, and educational resources to learn about cutting-edge research findings and best practices.
- **Beekeeping universities and programs:** Consider enrolling in online courses or workshops offered by universities specializing in beekeeping research and education.

Staying informed about new discoveries and advancements can help you make informed decisions and improve your beekeeping practices.

Beekeeping can be emotionally challenging, with potential for stress, anxiety, and even burnout. Remember:

- **Prioritize your well-being:** Seek support from friends, family, or mental health professionals if you're struggling.
- **Connect with the beekeeping community:** Share your experiences and find understanding and support from fellow beekeepers.
- **Practice self-care:** Find healthy coping mechanisms like spending time in nature, engaging in hobbies, or practicing mindfulness.

Taking care of yourself is crucial for sustained enjoyment and success in beekeeping. Remember, you're not alone, and seeking help is a sign of strength, not weakness.

By tapping into the wealth of resources and support available, you can navigate beekeeping challenges confidently, learn from others, and continue your journey towards becoming a successful and fulfilled beekeeper. Remember, the beekeeping community is here to support you every step of the way!

OUTRO

Congratulations! You've reached the end of this beekeeping journey, and with it, you've unlocked a world buzzing with wonder and purpose. The knowledge you've gleaned from these pages has equipped you with the essential tools and understanding to confidently step into the role of an apiarist. Remember, beekeeping is a lifelong learning adventure, but with the foundation you've built, you're well on your way to nurturing thriving hives and experiencing the immense satisfaction of coexisting with these fascinating creatures.

As you embark on this exciting new chapter, remember the core principles we've explored: respect, responsibility, and a deep appreciation for the delicate balance of the beehive ecosystem. Your gentle care and informed actions will not only benefit your bees but also contribute to the greater good. By choosing beekeeping, you've embraced a sustainable and profoundly impactful activity. Bees are the cornerstone of our ecological health, responsible for pollinating a third of the world's food supply. Through your dedication, you'll be actively participating in the preservation of biodiversity and ensuring the health of our planet for generations to come.

The journey ahead promises both challenges and triumphs. Embrace the inevitable learning curve, for each obstacle overcome will deepen your understanding and strengthen your bond with your bees. There will be moments of awe as you witness the intricate workings of the hive, moments of frustration when things don't go as planned, and moments of pure joy as you witness the fruits of your labor – the golden treasure of honey, the vibrant life teeming within your apiary.

Remember, the beekeeping community is here to support you every step of the way. Seek guidance from experienced beekeepers, share your experiences, and learn from each other. This shared passion for these extraordinary creatures creates a unique bond that transcends borders and backgrounds.

As you venture forth, I wish you nothing but success, fulfillment, and endless fascination in your beekeeping endeavors. May your hives hum with vitality, your honey be abundant, and your spirit be forever touched by the magic of the bees.

Thank you for choosing beekeeping, for choosing to make a difference, and for allowing me to be a part of your journey.

Warmly,

Don

ABOUT THE AUTHOR

From a young age, I've been captivated by the tiny marvels that are honeybees. Watching them flit between blooms, their fuzzy bodies buzzing with an infectious energy, instilled in me a deep appreciation for their intricate world. This fascination wasn't merely passive wonder; I spent countless hours alongside my father, helping him tend to his beehives. Witnessing his dedication to these creatures and the delicate balance of their ecosystem sparked a passion within me to learn everything I could about beekeeping.

Made in the USA
Columbia, SC
09 August 2024

40261660R00057